8 Streets to Christ

The Evidence for God and the Street Map to Heaven.

Brian Douglas Young

byoung8sts@gmail.com

Imprimatur:

Most Reverend James F. Checchio, JCD, MBA Diocese of Metuchen, NJ

Nihil Obstat:
Reverend John G. Hillier, Ph.D.
Censor Librorum

June 23, 2020

The Nihil Obstat and Imprimatur are official declarations that a book or pamphlet is free of doctrinal or moral error. No implication is contained therein that those who granted the Nihil Obstat and the Imprimatur agree with the contents, opinions, or statements expressed.

Contents

Introduction

How do you get to Heaven? By treating Earth as the stopover, *not* the vacation destination. Earth is where you must toil over loving matters and execute your life's mission; both can be achieved by traversing the 8 Streets to Christ, paved in the latter part of this book. Be assured, this journey will later yield a boarding pass on a connecting flight to Paradise.

This book also answers three questions: *Does God Exist?*, *Why am I here on Earth?*, and *How do I get to Heaven?* My belief is that if you act on these answers, you will later occupy the room that Jesus is preparing for you.

Why write this book? Atonement. I am ashamed to say that, despite best intentions, I failed to team up with my wife to help teach my three children about their faith – now they are grown. So, here it is. I hope that they will read it.

I began to write *8 Streets to Christ* only after reading through 3,000 religious pages, teaching religious education classes for six years, and listening (on my commute) to 72 religious CDs – *each* five times. (The intense CD listening sessions blew out three car audio players!) After three more years of research and daily prayers to God to *please* give me all the answers, this book came to fruition. If it fails, then *I* wrote it; if it succeeds, then *He* wrote it.

These nine years of seeking God brought still more personal shame for me. I found my character to be weaker than I thought. Condescending, prideful, and impatient, I should be entered into the record books under, "Most decades with little-to-no improvement in the category of *sinner.*" Yes, a sinner is this book's scribe; but the book's *answers* are from ones – and One – greater than I.

So, I come late to the table with respect to character and good parenting...but I am not dead yet. I now realize I am in the faith race of my life. I hope that you'll join me, as we boldly *run it to win it.*

Consider the faith race of this African man who refused to renounce Christ and was martyred. The letter that was found on him reads in part:

"I am a part of the fellowship of the Unashamed. I have the Holy Spirit Power. The die has been cast. I have stepped over the line. The decision has been made. I am a disciple of Jesus Christ.

My pace is set, my gait is fast, my goal is Heaven, my road is narrow, my way is rough, my companions few, my Guide is reliable, my mission is clear.

I won't give up, back up, let up, or shut up until I've preached up, prayed up, paid up, stored up, and stayed up for the cause of Christ. I must go until He returns, give until I drop, preach until all know, and work until He comes.

And when He comes to get His own, He will have no problem recognizing me.

My banner is clear: I am a part of the Fellowship of the Unashamed."

Question #1: *Does God Exist?*

If No → Then atoms and Adam; gravity and grizzlies; water, whales, plants and planets; human consciousness, DNA, and the universe(s) sprang from *Nothingness* and exist by pure chance, with no apparent *Cause*.

If Yes → Then the upcoming 25 phenomena have God as their *Cause*.

These miracles, sightings and other unexplainable events have been investigated by many scientists and experts, some of whom have concluded their studies by converting to Christianity... or fainting! One of the events described below was witnessed by 70,000 people.

With these things in mind, what are the odds for debunking *all* 25?

Topic #1: The Resurrection of Jesus Christ

The risen Lord affirms God's existence. But the naysayers to Jesus' Resurrection – and to Christianity, itself – cite five alternative explanations, marked by the SCHEME acronym, S-C-H-M-E: **S**woon, **C**onspiracy, **H**allucination, **M**yth, and **E**xistence. Each letter denotes an argument *against* the Resurrection.

Let's visit this scheme in reverse acronym order:

E – Existence: Did Jesus even exist?

- Tacitus, a Roman senator and historian, recorded what is considered the most important reference to Jesus outside the New Testament. Around AD 115: "...Christus, from whom the name [Christians] had its origin, suffered the extreme penalty during the reign of Tiberius at the hands of one of our procurators, Pontius Pilate, and a most mischievous *superstition* ...[was] checked for the moment ..." (The "superstition" was speculated to be that Jesus had been crucified but then rose from the grave.)
- Josephus, a non-Christian Jew, in AD 90s, also wrote of Pontius Pilate condemning Jesus to the cross.
- In AD 111, Roman politician, judge, and author, Pliny the Younger, mentioned Jesus as a Christian god.
- Gary Habermas, in *The Verdict of History*, details 39 ancient sources documenting Jesus' life, teachings, crucifixion, and resurrection.

So, we know that early Christians, as well as Jews and Romans, knew Jesus. No one has *disproved* His existence.

M – Myth: Could the Bible[1] account of a miracle-worker named Jesus, who rose from the dead, be a myth?

- A ***man-risen-from-the-dead*** myth would need time to develop in order to distance itself from witnesses who were alive during the time of Jesus and could have refuted the claim. But scholars believe that the *Rising* creed (1 Corinthians 15:3-8) was received by Paul from Peter and James merely three

---

[1] Don't believe in the Bible? Consider these points before casting a final judgment on it: It's not a book that fell from the sky. It's comprised of God-inspired, holy writings from about 40 persons [32 Old Testament and 8 New Testament authors] who lived over a span of 500+ years. The authors consistently describe a love story between God and humankind. The Bible is the most revered well-spring of truth and life instruction – there is no peer.

Read the Bible again – with fresh eyes.

to five years after the crucifixion. It was also discussed in St. Paul's letters written between AD 50–63. So, too, in Acts 2:32, Peter said, "God has raised Jesus to life, and we are all witnesses of it." In Acts 3:15, Peter also said, "You killed the author of life, but God raised Him from the dead. We are witnesses of this." Then, Peter to Cornelius "…[we] ate and drank with Him after He rose from the dead."

Paul's *Rising* creed also mentions specific individuals and groups – eye-witnesses – to whom the risen Lord had appeared. Non-believers then had in hand the suspects to pursue, question, arrest, and torture in order to squelch the *Rising* creed. But none of the eyewitnesses/believers ever changed their story.

- The Resurrection story gave women credit for being the first to discover the empty tomb. Women's testimony was worthless in AD 33, so why would the Gospel writers include this detail? The reason is that women *were* the first to see the empty tomb. The writers faithfully recorded what actually happened.
- Christ's enemies failed to produce His corpse – the displayed corpse would have busted the myth.

So the truth was simply being told: Jesus was crucified and then rose from the dead. No myth.

H – Hallucination: Did people see a hallucination of Jesus after His Resurrection?

- After Jesus rose, He was seen in 10 places by a collective 500 people over the course of 40 days. Appearances lasted for several minutes; sometimes more. Jesus also ate and was physically touched by some. Hallucinations normally last for only seconds and are not shared by people *across* appearances.
- Could Saul of Tarsus – an advocate for murdering Christians – have been converted to Paul of Christianity simply by seeing a hallucination? Think of what it would take for you to flip your strong beliefs on topics such as religion, politics, or *abortion*. No, a more impactful encounter would have been necessary to convert a religious zealot. Saul was blinded for three days, and received an in-Person, scolding from Jesus, Himself.

No hallucination.

C – Conspiracy: The apostles either stole the body of Jesus or lied about His Resurrection. Here are the two facets:

1)   Theft: In order to steal Jesus' body from the tomb, the apostles would need to silently roll away a boulder, enter the tomb, unwrap the body (discarded cloths were found in the empty tomb: John 20:6-7) and whisk it away, all in full view of soldiers who would, themselves, have faced death if the body were stolen. The unarmed apostles, carrying the body, would then need to overpower the guards to escape. On the other hand, the Romans or Jews would not have stolen the body either; they wanted to suppress the rise of Christianity.

Reality: Not even the most skeptical critic today believes that the body was stolen. The tomb, however, *had* to be empty in order to preach about Jesus' Resurrection in Jerusalem, near the site of the Crucifixion, where people were actively converting to Christianity.

2)   Lie: The apostles fabricated Jesus' Resurrection. Apostles, and disciples like Paul, preached Jesus' resurrection and the Good News.[2] For this, they were often ridiculed, beaten, and imprisoned. Some were executed:

- James the Greater, who continued to preach, was killed by a sword under Herod Agrippa in AD 44 (Acts 12:1-2). His death led to the departure of the rest of the apostles from Jerusalem.
- James the Lesser was stoned to death in AD 62. His death was reported by Josephus (a Jew) in AD 93/94, and by two Christian sources (Hegesippus, and Clement of Alexandria) and one Gnostic source (First Apocalypse of James) all within 100-150 years from the event.
- Peter, who three times denied knowing Jesus prior to His crucifixion, was threatened with death if he continued preaching about a risen Jesus. Peter persisted; so he then was sentenced to death and crucified as foretold by Jesus in John 21:18: "…when you are old, you will stretch out your hands and another will dress you and carry you where you do not want to go."
- Paul was killed and likely beheaded by Romans. This is inferred by Clement in a non-biblical reference (1 Clement 5:5-7), in AD 95/96. Prior to Paul's death, he was quoted in 2 Timothy 4:6-7, "For I am already being poured

---

[2] The Good News is contained in the Gospels: Jesus is God, and by His dying on the cross and His rising from the dead, He has given us a chance at eternal life in Heaven – if we would just imitate His life through our love of God and neighbor.

out as a drink offering, and the time of my departure has come. I have fought the good fight, I have finished the race, I have kept the faith." Paul also said in 2 Corinthians 11:24-25, "Five times at the hands of the Jews I received forty lashes minus one. Three times I was beaten with rods, once I was stoned, three times I was shipwrecked…"

If you were an apostle who conspired to say that (common man) Jesus rose from the dead, would you suffer and die for that lie? Peter Kreeft, professor of philosophy at Boston College, summarizes the argument against a conspiracy: "Nothing proves sincerity like martyrdom. The change in [the apostles'] lives from fear to faith, despair to confidence, confusion to certitude, runaway cowardice to steadfast boldness under threat and persecution, not only proves their sincerity but testifies to some powerful cause. Can a lie cause such a transformation?" J.P. Moreland, PhD, said this: "…11 credible people with no ulterior motives, with nothing to gain, or lose [except their lives!], who all agree they observed something miraculous – now you've got some difficulty explaining that away."

Seeing a *risen* Lord is the only plausible reason some of them went to their cruel deaths.

S – Swoon: Jesus didn't die. Roman soldiers failed to crucify Him. These scenarios make death inevitable:

- Alexander Metherell, MD, PhD, said this of Roman, pre-crucifixion torture: "As the flogging continued, the lacerations would tear into the underlying skeletal muscles and produce quivering ribbons of bleeding flesh." Further, a 3rd-century historian, Eusebius, said this about Roman floggings: "The sufferer's veins were laid bare, and the very muscles, sinews, and bowels of the victim were open to exposure."
- Roman soldiers were under a penalty of death if they failed to crucify any condemned person.
- Pilate put *INRI* (meaning "Jesus of Nazareth, King of the Jews") above the cross (in three languages) to warn others of what would befall them if they claimed to be a king. So, that upped the ante that Jesus' crucifixion would not fail.
- John 19:33-34: "But when they came to Jesus and saw that he was already dead, they did not break his legs, but one soldier thrust his lance into his side, and immediately blood and water flowed out." The latter, clear, watery fluid

was from pericardial effusion (around the heart) and the pleural effusion (fluid around the lungs) – both of these are produced by a failing heart.

The *SCHME* is defeated. Still skeptical of Jesus' Resurrection? Read on.

Resurrection Aftershocks:

The Jews in Jesus' time were aware of their tragic (1,000+ year) past, and their current lot: first they were Egyptian slaves; then Israeli victims of the Neo-Assyrian Empire; then deportees to Babylon; now subjects of Roman rule. So, Jewish norms and beliefs were extremely important to the Jewish people as a way to preserve their identity and avoid disappearing altogether. Jews also believed that abandoning their beliefs would risk their souls being damned to hell after death. But weeks after Jesus was crucified, over 10,000 Jews were following Him as the leader of a new religion!

Jews are suddenly giving up five of the vital social and theological structures that they had been taught since childhood. Jewish institutions were being toppled. For example:

- No more yearly animal sacrifices to remove a person's sins.
- A 1,500-year tradition of keeping the Sabbath on Saturdays is abruptly moved to keeping Sundays holy because that was the day Jesus rose from the dead.
- Believing in a monotheistic God was now changed to believing in the Holy Trinity God: one God in three Persons.

Something very big was going on here! What could *possibly* cause it? Nothing **less** than seeing the risen Jesus could shake up 1,500-year-old traditions.

The Resurrection Verdict:

"[Do we] know enough about the universe to say that God … can never break into our world in a supernatural way [by raising someone from the dead]?" [Gregory A. Boyd, PhD]

A flogging that exposed ribbons of quivering flesh… six-inch nails driven into His body… lifted vertically… lifted to hang on the cross… at 3 pm, death and a spear to the heart… buried… in three-days' time, an empty tomb!… Disciples willing to be killed rather than deny that He rose ... 10,000 Jews abandon 1,500-year traditions to follow Him under a new religion. What else supports all the evidence *better* than the Resurrection?

Contemporary clincher: Sir Lionel Luckhoo, a successful lawyer, twice knighted by Queen Elizabeth, and Guinness Book of World Records holder as *Most Successful Lawyer* – with most consecutive murder acquittals (245) – applied the resurrection to his own rigorous analysis, and then said: "I say unequivocally that the evidence for the resurrection of Jesus Christ is so overwhelming that it compels acceptance by proof which leaves absolutely no room for doubt."

TRUTH: Jesus is God, He is resurrected, and is now sitting at the right hand of the Father awaiting your prayers and longing for a personal relationship with you.

Topic #2: Our Lady of Fatima, May 13–October 13, 1917

Fatima, Portugal, 1917, in a field named Cova da Iria:

Three young shepherds – Jacinta and Francisco Marto, age 7 and age 9 and their cousin Lucia Santos, age 10 – describe visits from a Lady, "brighter than the sun", who appears and speaks to them while hovering over a small oak tree. The visits occur on the 13th of every month from May until October.

The children are accompanied by 50 people in June; 5,000 in July; and exponentially more in the ensuing months. The witnesses could not see the lady's image, but described a small greyish cloud or a ball of light that comes and settles over the tree. Some reported: "There was only one mysterious effect to support our impression of another presence there. We heard something buzzing like a small, small voice, but could not understand what it was trying to say."

The Lady's July 13th visit is detailed:
- She gives the children three secrets.
- She states that she will do several things on October 13th: "…I will tell you who I am and what I want. I will then perform a miracle so that all may believe."
- She reveals secret #1 to the young shepherds: "The Lady opened her hands, as she had in the preceding months, but instead of the glory and beauty of God that her opened hands had shown us before, we now were able to behold a sea of fire. Plunged in this flame were devils and souls that looked like transparent embers; others were black or bronze, and in human form, [floating about in the conflagration] …and amid cries of pain and despair, which horrified us so that we trembled with fear. The devils could be distinguished from the damned human souls by the terrifying forms of weird and unknown animals in which they were cast." Witnesses notice Lucia gasp in sudden horror during the July visit and attribute her reaction to this revelation.
- In secret #2, the Lady says that if people do not stop offending God that there will be an even more terrible war – and it will begin soon after a "strange and unknown light" is seen in the sky.
- Secret #3 reveals a prediction on the death of a pope.

The July visit concludes with the Lady departing into the eastern sky.

Fatima neighbors hearing of the events in the field but not present at Cova da Iria scoff and rain down ridicule upon the three children. The situation reaches a climax in early August when Fatima's district Administrator kidnaps the children in an attempt to learn the secrets and force them to admit that their story is a lie. He first puts them in the local jail with its resident criminals and threatens them with submersion in boiling oil. The three still do not change their story. Jacinta is pulled from the cell first and dragged away to die. The other two could hear her screaming, but they do not change their stories. Next to be taken from the cell is Francisco, then, later, Lucia; still they do not waver. Lucia enters the vat room and finds both cousins alive; so the threat was a ruse. The Administrator is shocked that death, itself, can't deter the three from what they have seen and heard out in the field.

The children are hounded by questions daily. Some are formal inquiries like those conducted by Dr. Manuel Formigao. He questions each child independently, with consistent, specific and often tricky or misleading questions. He repeats this process over and over. All the children's answers align, except for one question: When will the current World War end? One shepherd indicates the Lady says that day; another says that it will end soon. But, except for this one trivial point, the *consistency* is overwhelming and too much to bear for Dr. Formigao. He abandons his inquiry and accepts that the predicted October 13th miracle – if it happens – will settle the entire issue.

On October 13th, Fatima has driving rains. About 70,000 spectators, soaked and ankle-deep in mud, arrive at noon to witness the miracle. Among the crowds are the shepherds' families. They fear for the safety of their children should no miracle occur. But the three shepherds are unafraid; they know what they have seen and what has been promised by the Lady.

It's 1:30 PM, with rain near its end, and still no visit or miracle. Some are pressing the children for when…WHEN? It's then that Lucia sees the lightning that typically precedes visits. The Lady appears, at the *true* noon time, at the sun's zenith. One witness sees a column of thin, bluish smoke, about two meters long directly over the children. Our Lady reveals herself as the *Lady of the Rosary* – the Virgin Mary, the Mother of God, and the Mother of Jesus. She also says, "People must amend their lives and ask pardon for their sins. They must not offend our Lord any more, for He is already too much offended!" She departs to the east, and while leaving, raises her palms to the clouded sky.

Then it occurs: the clouds disappear and the miracle of the sun begins. For 10 minutes the sun spins, drops towards the earth, and returns to its original position, defying the laws of physics. It bathes the earth in various colors. Witnesses notice that the ground and their clothes are completely dry. Engineers studying this case later say that an incredible amount of energy was imparted to the pools of water and heavy clothing to dry it all in 10 minutes' time. The non-Catholic secular newspapers describe the events as being supernatural. Skeptics, atheists, and believers alike all know they have just witnessed a miracle.

Here are other facts on the supernatural *miracle-of-the-sun*:
- It also was seen far from the Cova da Iria by spectators 11 and 40 miles away. Some thought the world was coming to an end.
- The multitudes in Cova da Iria were seized with terror as the sun appeared to fall towards the earth. There were simultaneous cries of affliction, prayers, and people dropping to their knees. As the sun returned to its normal position, the people were relieved that the catastrophe was averted.
- Some were miraculously cured of their ailments after eating the dirt near the small oak tree. Water that bubbled up from a hole dug near the tree resulted in more cures for those who drank it. Father John De Marchi states, "There is clinical certainty that at Fatima the blind have had sight restored, while men and women stretcher-borne have risen from their litters to cry hosannas to the Power that can, in one moment, banish cancer, loosen the fist of the tightest paralysis, or render whole and clean the shrunken lungs of abandoned tuberculars. More than a hundred contradictions of the natural physical law have been registered at Fatima and held to be valid only after the most exhaustive and scrupulous examination of all available evidence. The author has himself been present at many miraculous cures…"

The Fatima visits are supported by other events:
- Nearly 20 years after the sighting, Lucia witnessed the "strange and unknown light" as foretold in 1917 by Our Lady to be the precursor to an even more terrible war. It was January 24, 1938, when an aurora borealis occurred as far south as southern Australia. A headline in the *New York Times* read: "Aurora borealis startles Europe. People flee, call firemen." World War II followed a year later.
- Our Lady, the Virgin Mary, foretold Jacinta's and Francisco's early deaths and said that Lucia would remain to relay the Fatima story and its messages to the world. Francisco died 18 months later, in 1919, at age 10, and Jacinta died 28 months later, in 1920, at age 9 – both from the 1918 flu epidemic. Lucia lived to almost 98 years old, dying in 2005.

- One of the Lady's secrets referred to a vision of the death of a Pope. On the Feast Day of Our Lady of Fatima, May 13th, 1981, Pope John Paul II was shot. He didn't die, and he later traveled to Fatima to thank the Virgin Mary for sparing his life.

A closing thought: Hundreds of witnesses gave testimony to the October 13th events and the unnatural solar activity. They were believers and non-believers, pious old ladies and scoffing young men. But for those still confident that a natural explanation will be found for the events of October 13th, 1917, ponder this: the *miracle of the sun* was predicted in July, 1917, and viewed by thousands in October on the exact day and exact hour predicted. *That* alone is a miracle and lends credence to all that happened in 1917, in the shepherd field at Fatima.

One hundred years have passed. What was once a peaceful meadow, teaming with sheep, has become a sea of devotion and love for Immaculate Mary, the Mother of God.

Topic #3: The Shroud of Turin

The Shroud of Turin is a burial cloth bearing the life-size image of a crucified man and perfectly aligns with Christ's crucifixion. Could this be Jesus's burial cloth or is it a forgery? This debate is what makes the Shroud of Turin the most studied object in human history. Let's look at the evidence:

The case for forgery ➔ The Shroud's 1988 radiocarbon dating says it was made around the 14th century AD and was most likely produced in Europe. That's the only evidence in support of a fake.

But the evidence *against* the accuracy of the radiocarbon dating procedure is overwhelming:

- Only one sample from the Shroud was removed and tested – accurate scientific carbon dating requires the testing of multiple samples.
- The sample was contaminated with a microorganism coating.
- The Shroud was in the 1532 fire in Chambery, France, which slightly altered its carbon content.
- The greatest contradiction to the Shroud's alleged 14th century radiocarbon date is the Sudarium of Oviedo, a 3-ft by 2-ft piece of linen cloth, thought to have covered the head of Jesus immediately after His crucifixion. The Sudarium (Facecloth) does not display an image, but its markings and stains are consistent with the Shroud as well as Scripture accounts of Christ's torture and execution. Both linens must have touched the same face. Just the facts:
  - The Facecloth and Shroud both contain male blood of rare type *AB* and the same plant aloes.
  - The Facecloth and the Shroud have over 100 blood spots that match exactly.
  - The length of the nose is equal on both.
  - The blood stains from the thorns on the nape of the neck match on both artifacts.
  - The forehead blood stains caused by the crown of thorns match in both linens.
  - The Gospel of John 20:6-7 supports the existence of the artifacts: "When Simon Peter arrived after him, he went into the tomb and saw the burial cloths there, and the cloth that had covered his head, not with the burial cloths but rolled up in a separate place."
  - Both artifacts contain the same rare pollen only found in Israel.

- o Many scientists say that the odds are virtually 100% that the Facecloth and Shroud were used on the same crucified person.
- o The Facecloth is dated AD 616. Its perfect alignment with the Shroud markings thus *proves* a Shroud origination date to be much earlier than the 14th century date.

Let's take it a step further. Here are the job skills required to produce a 14th century forgery of the Shroud of Turin:

- Holographer: The forger would have to know how to produce an X-ray, holographic (3-dimensional) image like that on the Shroud. Holography did not exist until the invention of the laser in the 1960s, 600 years after the supposed forgery date.
- Energy scientist: Twenty-first century scientists say that they would need about 14,000 lasers to produce the Shroud's image. Researcher Dr. Paolo Di Lazarro notes the ultraviolet light necessary to form the image exceeds the maximum power released by all known ultraviolet light sources.
- Botanist: A forger would need to know the unique characteristics of pollen from different regions of the world in order to determine how much exposure the Shroud would need in Jerusalem to dupe scientists into thinking it was the real thing.
- Linguist and seer: A holographic image of the Shroud revealed three Hebrew letters on a small oval plaque under the crucified man's beard. Would a European forger have known how to create and obscure this symbol with the foreknowledge that holograms would later be invented to reveal the image?
- Bible and Roman historian: The back image on the cloth of the crucified man contains marks, each the exact size of the bone or iron ends of a *flagrum*, an instrument used by Romans to whip their prisoners. The historian/forger would have to be familiar with the structure of the flagrum (three strings, each with a bone/iron end) and the maximum number of times it was allowed to be used (40). So, 40 lashes times 3 bones = 120 marks, which is the exact number found on the image of the man's back on the Shroud. Also, Jesus' crucifixion was not typical of the ones carried out by Roman soldiers. Jesus was crowned with thorns, flogged and pierced in the side by a spear. Also, His legs were not broken. Roman soldiers normally broke the crucified person's legs to hasten death.
- Anatomist: a person producing the Shroud had to have known that a nail through the palm couldn't support the body weight of the one crucified – the nail had to be applied through the wrist, which is exactly how it exists on

the Shroud. Also, when nailing through the wrist, the thumbs naturally turn inward. The thumbs on the Shroud indeed are missing.

- Artist with excellent spatial relations skills and surgical precision: Scientists have determined that all the blood stains on the Shroud exist under the image and no trace image exists under the blood. It would take the greatest (or luckiest) artist to perfectly place blood first, and then image second.

- Jewish undertaker: The Shroud shows evidence of at least 11 different ancient Jewish customs and burial practices. Could a Middle Ages forger have done time as a Jewish undertaker, too?

The case for Jesus Christ's burial cloth ➔

Here is additional evidence supporting the Shroud's authenticity:

- Contemporary tests date the Shroud to around AD 1st century: Dr. Raymond Roger's vanillin test puts the Shroud between 1,300 and 3,000 years old. Dr. Giulio Fanti's cellulose degradation test puts the Shroud between 700 BC and AD 100. And Fanti's tensile strength test of the fibers predicted their origin to be between AD 1 and AD 800. On average these new tests show an origination date between 283 BC and AD 217.

- A pollen test by Swiss Botanist Max Frei found 45 out of 58 pollen grains are from Israel – 13 of these 45 grains being unique to Israel and found at the bottom of the Dead Sea and the Sea of Galilee.

- Dr. John Jackson on the Shroud's creation: "…an intense burst of…ultraviolet radiation produced…a perfect three-dimensional negative image …of the body wrapped in it." Further, "we know of no *natural* explanation for the Shroud's [front and back body] image combined with the interior (skeletal) and exterior image of the hands." Finally, "…all we can do is eliminate every *known* natural cause of this seemingly unique radiation. The uniqueness and current inexplicability of this phenomenon gives us reason to *believe* that God has given us evidence of Jesus' resurrection."

The Sudarium Facecloth is a testimony to Jesus' passion and death on the cross, while the Shroud's mysteriously formed image is a testimony to His Resurrection. We continue to learn new things about the Shroud of Turin, and these things keep pointing to a Shroud creation date around the 1st century AD.

Luke 8:17: "For nothing is hidden that will not become evident, nor anything secret that will not be known and come to light."

Topic #4: The Cloak of Guadalupe

December 8th, 1531, Guadalupe, Mexico:

A humble peasant named Juan Diego meets Mary, the Mother of God. She requests that a church be built on Tepeyac Hill, where Aztecs had earlier worshipped their earth goddesses. Juan tells the local bishop, but Bishop Zumarraga first wants proof of Mary's visit before he acts. Juan tells Mary of the bishop's want, and she then directs him to collect roses as proof of her visit. Roses don't grow in Guadalupe in December, but Juan still finds them and gathers them into his cloak, a cactus-fiber outer garment, called a *tilma*. He revisits the bishop and opens his tilma. The roses drop – and so do the bishop and others – to their knees. The roses are nothing compared to the group's discovery of an Image of Our Lady on Juan's tilma.

It then begins. The tilma's Image of Our Lady is viewed by Aztec natives – who just decades before gave to their gods a regular offering of human blood, sacrificing thousands. They now, instead, convert to Catholicism, on average about 3,000 per day, every day, for seven years. About eight million become Catholic, which is the majority of all Mexicans in 1531. This is the largest mass conversion in the history of the world. The tilma today is enshrined in a Mexico City basilica and is the most visited Catholic pilgrimage site in the world.

Did the Virgin Mary truly visit Guadalupe in 1531? You judge:

- NASA scientists cannot explain how the Image was imprinted on the tilma. And there are no brush strokes: "She's imprinted like a photo," says Nydia Alatorre, director of the basilica museum.
- Cactus fiber tilmas last about 15 years – Our Lady's tilma was left out in the open air for more than a century, vulnerable to dirt and smoke, and physically touched by thousands. The tilma is still around today after almost 500 years and its original Image shows no signs of wear.
- 1785: powerful nitric acid is spilled on the Image, which should have destroyed the delicate cactus fibers. But the Image survives, undamaged with just an outer cloth stain.
- 1921: A bomb comprised of 29 sticks of dynamite is set off by terrorists near the Basilica's altar. A cast-iron cross is twisted out of shape and the marble altar rail is heavily damaged, but the Image and the glass surrounding it both remain untouched.
- The Image slightly changes colors depending on the angle at which a person views it; this effect only occurs in nature.

- The stars on Our Lady's clothing match exactly the constellations on that day in 1531.
- 1956: ophthalmologist Dr. Javier Torroella Bueno, MDS, discovers a triple reflection in the Image's eyes, characteristic of live human eyes.
- 1970s: A Japanese optician faints while examining the eyes. When he recovers, he said that, "the eyes were alive and looking at him."
- 1979: Biophysicist Phillip Callahan notices that the tilma remains at a constant temperature – 98.6° F – the temperature of a living human being.
- 1979: Dr. Jose Aste Tonsmann, PhD at IBM, produces a very high-resolution photograph of Our Lady's eyes from the tilma's Image, and he identifies in both eyes the same image of what appears to be an Indian, Bishop Zumarraga, the translator, Juan Diego showing the tilma, and a small family, about 10 people in all. The eyes of Our Lady appear to contain a photograph of those who were present in Bishop Zumarraga's office back in 1531.

A final thought:

Since the 16th century, the Catholic Church has a strict *miracle* vetting process. There have been over 2,000 alleged sightings of the Virgin Mary since AD 40, and only 16 have been deemed worthy-of-belief by the Church. Our Lady of Guadalupe is acknowledged as one of the 16 supernatural sightings – Our Lady of Fatima is another.

Topic #5: Our Lady of Lourdes

February 11, 1858, Lourdes, France:

Fourteen-year-old Bernadette Soubirous is out gathering firewood with her sister and a friend when she sees a beautiful "small young lady" hovering over a rose bush in the Grotto of Massabielle, just outside Lourdes. Bernadette has 18 visits from the lady that year, who eventually reveals herself as the *Immaculate Conception* – a term first ever used four years earlier by Pope Pius IX to describe the Virgin Mary, the Mother of God. Some other visits that year are telling:

- 3rd visit (18 Feb.): The Lady speaks for the first time, and she promises Bernadette – a cholera and extreme asthma sufferer – to be happy, not in this life but the next. "Would you have the goodness to come here for fifteen days?", she says to Bernadette. Observers notice this formal language is unusual when speaking to a penniless, working-class, peasant girl such as Bernadette.
- 9th visit (25 Feb.): The Lady appears and asks Bernadette to drink water located under a rock. The quantity of muddy puddle water is only a handful, but Bernadette drinks it. A spring begins to flow from the spot a day later.
- 12th visit (1 March): About 1,500 people are present. A nine-month pregnant woman who has a paralyzed arm from an accident reported a full recovery after bathing her arm in the spring.
- 16th visit (25 March): Bernadette asks the Lady 3 times who she is, but only gets a smile from her. Bernadette asks a 4th time, and the Lady then looks up to Heaven and says, "I am the Immaculate Conception."

The 17th appearance (7 April):

Dr. Pierre Romaine Dozous, the town physician, originally watches the apparitions from a skeptical viewpoint. He knew Bernadette well, and believes that she is in her right mind aside from the apparitions. He reports:

"Bernadette seemed to be even more absorbed than usual in the Appearance upon which her gaze was riveted. I witnessed, as did also everyone else there present, the fact which I am about to narrate. She was on her knees saying with fervent devotion the prayers of her Rosary which she held in her left hand while in her right was a large blessed candle, alight. The child was just beginning to make the usual ascent on her knees when suddenly she stopped and, her right hand joining her left, the flame of the big candle passed between the fingers of the latter. Though fanned by a fairly strong breeze, the flame produced no effect upon the skin which it was touching. Astonished at this strange fact, I forbade anyone there to interfere, and taking my watch in my hand, I studied the phenomenon attentively for a quarter of an hour. At the end of this time Bernadette, still in her ecstasy, advanced to the upper part of the Grotto, separating her hands. The flame thus ceased to touch her left hand. Bernadette finished her prayer and the splendor of the transfiguration left her face. She rose and was about to quit the Grotto when I asked her to show me her left hand. I examined it most carefully but could not find the least trace of burning anywhere upon it. I then asked the person who was holding the candle to light it again and give it to me. I put it several times in succession under Bernadette's left hand she drew it away quickly, saying 'You are burning me!' I record this fact just as I have seen it without attempting to explain it. Many persons who were present at the time can confirm what I have said."

The visits from the Mother of God conclude on July 16th. Bernadette that day remarks, "She was more beautiful than ever."

Did the Virgin Mary visit Lourdes in 1858? You decide:

- Others drank from the newly flowing spring in the grotto and many ailment cures were reported. At present at least 69 miracles – healings found to be beyond medical explanation – have been attributed to the waters at Lourdes. Countless miracle cures have been documented and verified by the independent Lourdes Medical Bureau, and the Church claimed that they were "extremely rigorous scientific and medical examinations," and no one has been able to explain what caused the cures. These healings were of nervous disorders and cancers to cases of paralysis and even blindness.

- The Lourdes Commission ran an analysis on the spring water: the only thing it revealed was a high mineral content. Bernadette believed faith and prayer and contact with the holy waters were all responsible for the cures.

- Church authorities and the French government rigorously interviewed Bernadette, and by 1862 they confirmed that she spoke the truth. The local bishop declared, "The Virgin Mary did appear indeed to Bernadette Soubirous."

- Bernadette died in 1879 while praying the Rosary. Her body was exhumed in 1925. It was found to be internally incorrupt. Dr. Comte comments, "What struck me during this examination, of course, was the state of perfect preservation of the skeleton, the fibrous tissues of the muscles (still supple and firm), of the ligaments, and of the skin, and above all the totally unexpected state of the liver after 46 years. One would have thought that this organ, which is basically soft and inclined to crumble, would have decomposed very rapidly or would have hardened to a chalky consistency. Yet, when it was cut it was soft and almost normal in consistency. I pointed this out to those present, remarking that this did not seem to be a natural phenomenon."

Our Lady of Lourdes is among the 16 Marian apparitions deemed worthy-of-belief. Lourdes has become one of the world's leading Catholic Marian shrines. An estimated 200 million people – equal to Brazil's 2015 population – have visited the shrine since 1860.

Topic #6: Stigmata

Stigmata are body marks similar to the crucifixion wounds of Jesus Christ. Stigmata primarily appear on a person's hands and feet. St. Paul in his letter to the Galatians refers to stone or flog marks he received from angry crowds who rejected his Gospel teachings: "I bear on my body the marks of Jesus." St. Francis of Assisi was the first witnessed stigmatic, and women comprise 80% of stigmatics.

Some wounds have exhibited themselves as a crown of thorns on the head or scourge marks on the back – and even a lance piercing on the side. Some people have faked their stigmata, so care is taken here to present only witness accounts and other facts. Are stigmata marks supernatural? You judge:

- St. Francis received, "…the gift of the five wounds of Christ", as witnessed by a Brother Leo, on September 14, 1224, on Mount Alverna, Italy, during a 40-day fast and retreat. Many others witnessed St. Francis's 5 wounds, including his companions, Brother Elias and St. Bonaventure. St. Francis probably received these wounds because he meditated more than anyone else on the Passion and crucifixion of Christ.

- In 2002, a psychoanalytic study suggested that stigmata may result from post-traumatic stress symptoms expressed in unconscious self-mutilation by abnormal autosuggestibility. More clearly, some physiologists maintain that persons impressed by the sufferings of Christ might themselves naturally produce bloody wounds on their body by using their imagination coupled with lively emotions. Facts and reality:

  o Sweating blood (called hematidrosis) is a very rare condition. The main causes: excessive exertion or severe stress. But even if we also include *ecstasy* or *hypnosis* as (unproven) causes of blood-sweating, no one would further argue that the blood-sweating could also be directed by the mind to occur in *specific areas* of the body similar to that of a crucified Christ.

  o Producing stigmata and its oozing blood on a weekly schedule, for years, must be supernatural – an example being St. Catherine de Ricci, whose ecstasies of the Passion lasted exactly 28 hours, every Thursday noon till Friday at 4 o'clock, for 12 years. On coming out of the ecstasy, her limbs were covered with wounds produced as if by whips or cords.

  o People are known to have produced fake or self-inflicted stigmata. But for most analyzed, true stigmatics, the Catholic Encyclopedia states, "…physicians have always taken measures to avoid these sources of error, proceeding with great strictness, particularly in modern times. Sometimes the patient has been watched night and day; sometimes the limbs have been enveloped in sealed bandages. Mr. Pierre Janet placed on one foot of a stigmatic a copper shoe with a window in it through which the development of the wound might be watched, while it was impossible for anyone to touch it."

- Dr. A. Imbert-Gourbeyre in 1894 counted 321 stigmatics in whom there are reasons to believe in a Divine action. The counts have risen since then.

- Christ died at age 33. There are at least nine stigmatic people with the wounds of Christ who also died at 33. This age of death may seem coincidental, but given the fact that people who at least attained the age of 21 during the Middle Ages averaged lifetimes into their 60s, death at age 33 is unusual and causes us to pause: could it be additional evidence that stigmata are from God?

- 20th century stigmatic, Marie-Rose Ferron, discovered the year of her death seven years prior to it. While in ecstasy on April 13, 1929, with visitors present, Rose asked Jesus how much longer she is to suffer, and then repeated aloud the answer, "Seven years!" She then died in May, 1936, at age 33.

- Physicians have discovered that they cannot cure the stigmata wounds with remedies. And, unlike natural wounds, stigmata wounds do not put forth a fetid odor, rather, sometimes they smell like perfume, as with those of Franciscan prioress, Juana of the Cross, or Blessed Lucy of Narni, Italy.

- Padre Pio, 1887-1968, claimed to have stigmata for 50 years, but was accused of faking it by potentially applying carbolic acid to his own skin. Yet in 2008 when his body was exhumed, not a trace of the stigmata was found. So how could carbolic acid be applied for years but later show no trace?

In 2008, the Catholic Congregation for the Doctrine of the Faith unsealed the 1921 investigation on Pio's stigmata, on which the late Bishop Carlo Raffaello Rossi ran the proceedings:

o His investigation ran for eight days, and he found Padre Pio to be a great man (not a gossiper) who spent 10-12 hours a day hearing confessions and celebrating Mass with great devotion.

- o But eight days' observation was not enough, so he asked 142 questions of Padre Pio while the Padre was under oath with his hand on the Gospels. Questions such as, "Who gave you the stigmata? For what reason? Were you given a specific mission?" were answered sincerely and summarily with it being "Jesus' desire."
- o Still not content, Bishop Rossi asked to examine the wounds. He saw that the wound in his side "changed aspects frequently and at that moment was in the shape of a triangle, never before seen." Bishop Rossi concluded that the wounds "of true stigmata were found in those of Padre Pio."
- o Another interesting fact on this stigmatic: Padre Pio's body temperature was witnessed multiple times by Father Lorenzo of San Marco, to be 109, 113, and 118.4° F – whereas 107 would normally kill a healthy person.

Stigmata is unexplainable, and no experimental proof exists of the human imagination producing stigmata – either on command, or on-schedule, or on specific body parts, or producing certain shapes – while under stress, hypnosis or ecstasy. It is a true mystery.

Topic #7: Miracle of Lanciano

Lanciano, Italy, AD 700s:

A monk is saying Mass. At the moment of Consecration when the bread and wine truly become Jesus' Body and Blood, the monk is plagued by persistent doubt.

Let's step back in time to recall the same moment in the first Mass on earth – the Last Supper – where Jesus said, "This is my Body…" and "This is my Blood…" In his Bread of Life Discourse, John 6:22-71, John the apostle noted that Jesus explained in different ways: "…unless you eat the flesh of the Son of Man and drink his blood, you do not have life within you." The Catholic Church has, at its core, the belief that the bread (host) and wine, when consecrated, *truly* becomes Jesus. This moment is called Transubstantiation. Jesus did not say that the bread "is a symbol of Me" or "looks like My body", but said, "This *is* my body". He also spoke of it in the Discourse. Why say *this hard teaching* unless it were true, given it would certainly cost Him followers.

Back to the doubting monk: his unbelief is suddenly met with a stunning transition of host and wine into real human flesh and blood – the first Eucharistic miracle since Jesus' time. All present witness this miracle at Lanciano, Italy, where the flesh and blood still survive today, 1,200 years later.

The miracle of Lanciano is the first, and to many, the greatest Eucharistic Miracle of the Catholic Church. But here's the one argument against it: there is no visual proof showing the host and wine *transitioning* to these relics of flesh and blood. Some say: no *visual*, no *miracle*. What say you on whether the following is convincing evidence for this miracle?

First, the groundwork:

- The resultant flesh and blood, the *relics*, can be traced through time. The miracle occurred in the Church of St. Legontian, Lanciano (nee Anxanum), Italy, in the 8th century. The relics were in the custody of the Basilian monks until 1175, Benedictine monks until 1252, and, since then, the Franciscans. In 1258, St. Francis of Assisi coordinated the building of a new church on the site, which would house the relics. A stone tablet, circa 1631, describes the miracle. The relics were then kept in the Valsecca Chapel from 1636 until

1902. Today, they are kept in a monstrance[3] at the Church of San Francesco, Lanciano.

- Tests on the relics have been recorded: The flesh and blood were examined immediately after the miracle. In 1574, the blood was tested by Archbishop Antonio Gaspar Rodriquez in front of witnesses. The relics were scientifically examined in 1970-71 (and in 1981, with even more advanced medical technology), by Dr. Odoardo Linoli, professor of anatomy and pathological histology, chemistry and clinical microscopy, and head physician of the Arezzo hospital. He was assisted in the earlier study by Dr. Ruggero Bertelli, professor emeritus of human anatomy at the University of Siena. Their analyses were conducted with scientific precision, and Dr. Bertelli independently corroborated Dr. Linoli's findings. Microscopic photographs were also taken. The results show:

  o The Flesh is real flesh. The Blood is real blood.
  o The Flesh and the Blood belong to the human species.
  o The Flesh consists of the muscular tissue of the heart.
  o The Flesh has a myocardium (heart wall), endocardium, vagus nerve and left ventricle.
  o The Blood's type is AB, that which is found on the Shroud of Turin.
  o The Blood contains proteins in the same percentages as in fresh blood.

In May 2005, Dr. Linoli said that while studying the relics of the Eucharistic miracle of Lanciano: "I had in my hand the endocardium. Therefore, there is no doubt at all that it is cardiac tissue."

Here's further evidence of the supernatural within the Miracle of Lanciano:

- Professor Linoli asserted that the blood, if taken from a cadaver, would have deteriorated rapidly without the use of preservatives. These relics are certified centuries old, free of preservatives, and were not hermetically sealed in their containers. They were exposed to the action of air and bacteria for many centuries, so they should have disintegrated, but haven't. Stunningly, they still exhibit the same properties as fresh human blood and flesh.
- The Blood is still living, which is not scientifically explainable due to the fact that blood cannot live outside the body for more than a few hours without artificial means.

---

[3] A clear-glass receptacle in which the consecrated Host is exposed for adoration.

- Finally, the doctors both concluded that only the skill of a trained pathologist could have obtained such a flesh sample of the heart: a tangential cut of the heart, a round cut, thick on the outer edges and lessening gradually and uniformly to the central area. Could this have also been accomplished 1,200 years ago?

Eucharistic miracles dramatically remind us of the 2,000-year-old teaching that Jesus is truly present in the consecrated Host and wine. That is why at every Mass:

- The space around the altar – the Sanctuary – and the Tabernacle, are both sacred.
- You bless yourself with Holy Water, recalling your baptism, upon entering the Church.
- You genuflect before entering your pew.
- The priests and deacons show reverence at the foot of the Sanctuary when they process in.
- The lectors and the extraordinary ministers of Holy Communion show reverence when they come forward to serve.
- We all reverently and respectfully acknowledge the unique presence of our Lord, especially at the consecration and when He is in the Tabernacle behind the altar.

See the topic's references to view images of the miracle.

Topic #8: Eucharistic Miracle of Sokółka – AD 2008

St. Anthony's Church, Sokółka, Poland:

Father Filip Zdrodowski celebrates the October 12th morning Mass. During Communion, a consecrated Host falls from the hands of an assistant, Father Jacek, who is immediately notified about it by a woman waiting to receive Communion. Seeing the Host is dirty, Father Jacek places it in a small vessel with water and locks it in a safe for several days so it can dissolve. The water will then be poured out into a special drain. On October 19th, Sister Julia Dubowska opens the safe and finds the consecrated bread almost dissolved but also tightly interconnected to a strange red clot, what looks like a bloody piece of flesh. On October 30th, by order of the Archbishop Edward Ozorowski, Father Gniedziejko delicately removes the Host and red clot, places it on a white linen corporal and locks it in the Tabernacle. It is then that two world-famous scientists and specialists in pathological anatomy are consulted: Professors Maria Elżbieta Sobaniec-Łotowska and Stanisław Sulkowski. On January 7, 2009, a sample of the Host is taken to the University of Medicine of Bialystok and examined independently by the two professors. They issue a common declaration: "The sample sent for evaluation looks like myocardial [heart] tissue. In our opinion, of all the tissues of living organisms this is the one that resembles it the most."

Summary details:

- A consecrated Host was transformed into a fragment of muscle tissue.
- It exhibits the agony of death, a severe stress as if on the point of cardiac arrest.
- Both professors carried out their studies independently using state-of-the-art light and electron microscopes and both came to the same conclusions.
- Professor Sulkowski says, "A consecrated Host quickly dissolves when immersed in water. But the Blessed Host from Sokółka has not broken down for reasons that remain baffling to science. What is still more remarkable is the fact that the middle portion of the Host turned into heart muscle tissue, forming an inseparable structure with the rest of the white Host."
- The photomicrographs are empirical, scientific proof that no one could have united the two structures – heart muscle tissue and bread. Even scientists equipped with the most up-to-date technology could not produce anything like it, so closely is the matter of the Host united and interpenetrated with

the heart muscle fibers. Professor Maria Sobaniec-Łotowska affirms this: "Even the scientists of NASA, who have at their disposal the most modern analytical techniques, would not be able to artificially recreate such a thing."

- Professor Sobaniec-Łotowska stresses, "This extraordinary and mysterious interpenetration of the white Host's material with human heart muscle fibers was observed, examined, and photographed using both light and electron microscopy. The indication is that there could not have been any human intervention. Yet another extraordinary fact bears mentioning. The Host remained immersed in water for a considerable length of time, after which it was placed on the corporal. Yet our studies indicated none of the changes one would have expected of heart muscle fibers being immersed in water for so long a period. From the point of view of empirical research, we are unable to explain this fact. These are undoubtedly the most important studies I have conducted in my life. The results were shocking to me. They point to an extraordinary phenomenon, which from a scientific standpoint, is simply inexplicable."

- A special Ecclesiastical Commission convened by Archbishop Ozorowski on March 30, 2009, interrogated pathomorphology experts and all the witnesses, verifying the sincerity of their testimonies. The Ecclesiastical Commission then stated: "The Host from which the sample was taken for the examination is the same one that has been transferred from the sacristy to the tabernacle of the chapel in the rectory. The intervention of strangers was not observed."

The miracle's image was seen in the 2012 film, *JA JESTEM*. It's also seen here: https://aleteia.org/2017/09/23/the-eucharistic-miracle-of-sokolka-the-host-is-tissue-from-heart-of-a-dying-man/

A black-and-white photo of it is displayed on the next page.

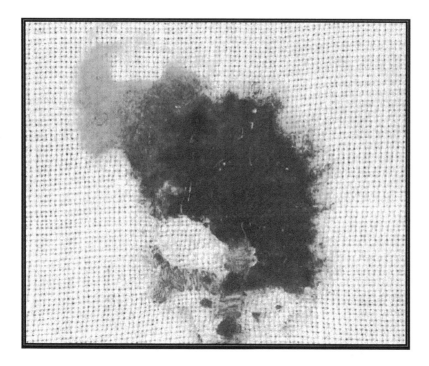

The Vatican International Exhibition's *Eucharistic Miracles of the World* has documented more than 130 worldwide Eucharistic miracles, similar to those of Lanciano and Sokółka. Common findings among the miracles: Host-made-flesh is heart muscle, the blood type is AB (the same as reported on the Shroud of Turin), the heart tissue has experienced great stress, and the miracles occurred in different locations with many different experts coming to the *same* conclusions.

Topic #9: Incorruptible Bodies

Bacteria on human bodies outnumber human cells about 3 to 1. About 100 trillion bacteria (3 pounds of them) also live in your intestines. So when we die, bacteria help decompose us from the inside out. It takes eight to 12 years for an unembalmed body in soil to become a skeleton, and up to 50 years if embalmed and in a coffin. Bacteria and time are the agents of decomposition. So when an unembalmed, unpreserved dead body does not succumb to its own bacteria after many years, it is an *incorruptible body*. These bodies remain virtually decay-free regardless of the number of gravedigger upheavals, delays in burial, temperature, moisture, application of decay accelerants like quicklime, or the physical proximity to other decaying corpses. Incorruptible bodies cannot be explained by reason or science, and they defy the laws of nature.

Incorruptible bodies:

- Have only occurred since Jesus' time.
- Remain flexible, not rigid or stiff.
- Sometimes have internal organs that remain supple after many years.
- Are a supernatural sign that the deceased lived a saintly life.
- Are mostly found to be sweetly smelling many years after death.
- Sometimes bleed or exude clear oils.
- Are unlike mummified or preserved bodies, which *are* stiff, discolored, skeletal, and malodorous.
- Are of devout Roman Catholics – over 250 of which are claimed by the Church. Interesting how a process of decay, devoid of intelligence, chooses to spare some, and only some who are Catholic. That, in itself, is a supernatural thing.

Some bodies are found partially incorrupt, with key parts remaining decay-free, like the heart or tongue. The latter case applies to St. Anthony of Padua, whose bones were exhumed in 1263, 32 years after his death. Although his body had turned to dust, his nearly 800-year-old tongue has survived and is on tour today; a miraculous sign of the saint's exceptional gift for preaching and teaching. This is truly unexplainable based on the fact that a human tongue, in life, is covered with bacteria, so it is quick to bloat and decompose after death.

Arguments against incorruptible bodies or body parts:

- Some dead bodies are not fully intact, so can they be deemed incorruptible?
- Some have a wax applied to their face, so they're not truly incorruptible.

These arguments are easily refuted:

- All living humans are loaded with bacteria. So, all unembalmed and unpreserved bodies should go skeletal in eight to 50 years. If a dead body shows only slight decay after 100 or more years, what explanation can science give for it? Currently none; so, it must be counted as incorruptible.

- Could placing a thin layer of wax on a *face* stop the rest of the body from decomposing? Of course not.

Finally, the incorruptibility of the bodies of certain saints further confirms the supernatural events in which they were involved such as the miracles of Fatima and Lourdes. Following are some examples:

- **Jacinta Marto** was canonized a saint on May 13, 2017, and was one of the three original visionaries at Fatima, Portugal, in 1917. She was born in 1910 and died in 1920. Twice exhumed, both in 1935 and 1951, her body was found to be incorrupt. Her tomb is in the Basilica of Our Lady of Fatima on the site where the children saw "a lady brighter than the sun." (See Topic 2: Our Lady of Fatima.)

- **St. Bernadette** was born Bernadette Soubirous in Lourdes, France. In 1858, she reported 18 apparitions of "a Lady". Bernadette died in 1879 and was exhumed three times by 1925. While her internal organs were found incorrupt, a light wax was required on face and hands to cover some discoloration. (See Topic 5: Our Lady of Lourdes.)

- **St. John Vianney** – He died in 1859 and was exhumed and found incorrupt in 1904. His body resides above the main altar in the Basilica at Ars in France.

- **Venerable Mary of Ágreda** died in 1665 and was discovered incorrupt when exhumed in 1909. The following was written about a second exhumation in 1989: "…a Spanish physician named Andreas Medina participated in another examination of the remains and told investigative journalist Javier Sierra in 1991: 'What most surprised me about that case is that when we compared the state of the body, as it was described in the medical report from 1909, with how it appeared in 1989, we realized it had absolutely not deteriorated at all in the last 80 years.'" Venerable Mary of Ágreda is credited with authoring the *Mystical City of God* through revelations from the Blessed Virgin. Mary of Ágreda's body has remained incorrupt for over 340 years and is kept in a convent in Spain. Read more about her in the upcoming topic of Bilocation.

Topic #10: Miraculous Crucifix of Limpias

Saint Peter's Church of Limpias – Santander, Spain, 1914-1921:

Automatons – human-like figures run by hidden mechanisms – were used in some churches in medieval times to impress peasant worshippers into believing in a supernatural power. So, could Leonardo da Vinci's 1495 plans for a human-like automaton have been used to build a robot over the altar at Saint Peter's Church? Let's see.

Saint Peter's is a 500-year-old church, and above its altar is a 6-foot *figure* of Jesus in His final moments of agony on the cross. The crucifix has been there since around 1776. This crucifix of Jesus is the subject of many humanoid apparitions:

- **August 1914**: Monk Don Antonio Lopez is asked to fix the electric light over the high altar. Up on the ladder for some time, his attention turns to the figure of Christ: "After I had worked for two hours, in order to rest myself a little, I began to clean the figure so that it could be seen more clearly. My head was on a level with the Head of the Christ, and at a distance of only a couple of feet from it…As I was gazing at the crucifix with the closest attention, I noticed with astonishment that Our Lord's eyes were gradually closing, and for five minutes I saw them quite closed."

  The monk is so startled by this that he loses his balance and falls from the ladder. Recovering, he later describes what happened to another church member, who also had heard that the figure of Christ closed His eyes at another time. This person suggests that the eyes must be controlled by some interior mechanism. But Don Antonio Lopez often cleans the crucifix, and examines its eyes: "…the eyes were so firmly fixed that even by pressing hard with one's fingers they could not be made to move in the least, nor could they be turned in any direction, as I have proved to myself again and again." He writes a report on the eyes closing and gives it to his superiors and says no more about it. His report isn't made public until March 16, 1920, after many other reported apparitions regarding the Crucifix of Limpias.

- **Sunday, March 30, 1919**: Mass and confessions are simultaneously in progress. A young girl enters the confessional of Father Jalon and tells him the eyes of Christ on the cross are closed. The priest ignores her sensational claim until other children also come to him with the same message. Later a parish priest sees the figure of Christ's eyes opening and closing and turning

His gaze from side to side – so the priest falls on his knees to pray. But his prayer is interrupted by the churchgoers, who declare that the figure is now perspiring. Father Jalon climbs up and sees perspiration covering the figure's neck and chest. After touching the neck, he notices that his fingers are wet from the fluid and shows his moistened fingers to the congregation. Another priest, Father Agatangelo later sees this miracle several times as he prays alone in the church at night.

- **Palm Sunday, April 13, 1919**: Two prominent men of Limpias enter the church and look upon the crucifix with initial thoughts of doubt – attributing sensational witness claims to hallucination or mass hysteria. One of them suddenly points upward as he sees the eyes actually moving and falls to his knees, crying for mercy and proclaiming his belief in the miracle.

- **Easter Sunday, April 20, 1919**: A group of nuns see both the eyes and lips of the figure move.

- **May 5, 1919**: Dr. Adolfo Arenaza gives testimony of seeing the eyes move four times while using his field glasses. He says: "Does our Lord really move his eyes? …I am of the opinion that he really does move them, for I have seen it myself."

- **August 4, 1919**: Rev. Valentin Incio of Gijon visits Limpias and writes of the miraculous crucifix: "At first our Lord seemed to be alive; His head then preserved its customary position…but His eyes were full of life and looked about in different directions… Now came the most touching moment of all. Jesus looked at all of us, but so gently and kindly, so expressively, so lovingly and divinely, that we fell on our knees and wept and adored Christ."

- **September 11, 1919**: Father Antonio de Torrelavega, "sees blood streaming from the left corner of Our Lord's mouth.", and the next day he states, "…several times He looked at me. Many other people who were kneeling round me also observed this…Now I verify it; there is no doubt the Santo Christo [crucifix] moves his eyes."

- **September 15, 1919**: The Coadjutor of St. Nicholas Church in Valencia, D. Paulino Girbes, was kneeling before the crucifix in the company of two bishops and 18 priests. He states: "We all saw the face of the Santo Christo become sadder, paler… The features at the same time took on the expression of a man who is in his death-struggle. This lasted a long time. I could not restrain my tears and began to weep…"

- **May 4, 1920**: A skeptical physician, Dr. Armando Penamaria, publishes a statement in the *La Montana* newspaper. The doctor describes what seemed to him to be, "...a re-enactment of Christ's death on the Cross." He first witnesses the figure's eyes and mouth movements, and he then changes positions twice in the church to verify the miracle. He says of the figure: "A moment later [Christ's] mouth was twisted sharply to the left, His...painfilled eyes gazed up to Heaven. His...lips appeared to tremble; the muscles of the neck and breast were contracted and made breathing forced and laboured. His...features showed the keenest pangs of death. His arms seemed to be trying to get loose from the cross with convulsive backward and forward movements and showed clearly the piercing agony that the nails caused in His hands at each movement. Then followed the indrawing of a breath, ...a frightful spasm, as with someone who is suffocating... at which the mouth and nose were opened wide. Now follows an outpouring of blood, fluid, frothing, that runs over the under-lip, and which the Saviour sucks up with His bluish, quivering tongue...then an instant of slight repose, another slow breath...the chest expands and contracts violently after which His head sinks limply on His breast, so that the back of the head can be seen distinctly. Then ... He expires! . . . I have tried to describe in outline what I saw during more than two hours..."

From 1914-1921, over 8,000 people recorded testimonies about the truth of the apparitions, and among those testimonies, 2,500 were sworn under oath. Among those who swore to an oath, or agreed to it if needed, were 13 doctors, five lawyers, four professors, three officers, two engineers, and others of various professions.

Some people believe that all these reported apparitions are fake. They cite three possible reasons: a) robotics, b) mass hallucination, and c) collusion by Saint Peter's Church priests and parishioners who probably drew attention to the church in order for it to be saved – for in 1919, it was almost deserted. Let's examine these arguments.

Collusion? ➔The population of Limpias was about 1,500 people between 1914 and 1921. Even if all decided to lie about the Crucifix of Limpias, would they have also been able to convince 6,500 more people to lie with them? Recall, 8,000+ testimonies were recorded.

Mass hallucination? ➔ Many apparitions occurred over the eight-year span. They happened day or night, and were seen by children and/or adults. In each of the occurrences, the audience consisted of from one to many people, with some individuals shifting their physical position in church in order to test the given apparition. Finally, the witnesses consisted of skeptical, medical, logical, spiritual, and educational people – more than 8,000. Does mass hallucination fit well here?

Robotics? ➔ Da Vinci's 1495 human robot plans described how to build a robot that could sit up, wave its arms, and move its head via a flexible neck while opening and closing its jaw. The Crucifix of Limpias' apparitions included the movement of eyes, lips, neck, torso, and limbs, with occurrences of bleeding, sweating, mouth froth, as well as sad and joyful expressions produced by the eyes. Could the figure of Christ hanging in the church since 1776 be an actual robot capable of *all* these things? And, a robot that could go undetected from close range by 8,000 people in an eight-year period?

What do you think?

Topic #11: Bilocation

Bilocation is a miraculous gift that enables an individual to be in two places at once. It occurs when the holy person feels the need to perform an act of mercy or charity for others who are far away. There are documented cases for Hindus, Christians, and Buddhists. But no scientific explanation has been found.

Skeptical? Most are. But consider these three examples among the many documented cases. The last case presented here is perhaps the most mysterious bilocation of them all.

Palace of Goti, Arezzo, Italy, September, 1774

Bishop Alphonsus de' Liguori says morning Mass on September 21, in Arezzo, Italy, then goes to his palace room, slumps into his armchair and begins to meditate. He remains motionless throughout the day and night and into the next morning, according to his companion, Reverend Tannoia, and the servants who remain near his door. The bishop's prolonged ecstasy finally breaks at 7AM, on September 22. He rings a bell to alert his staff of his wish to say Mass. Everyone who hears the bell comes running into his room. Surprised, he asks, "What is the matter?" They answer, "This is the second day that you have not spoken, eaten, nor given any sign of life." "You are right," said Bishop Alphonsus, "But you do not know that I have been assisting the pope, who has just died [today]."

Wait. Rome is 135 miles away and the *telegraph* doesn't exist yet – so how could Bishop Alphonsus know of the pope's death in Rome that very same day? The Arezzo monks only receive official news of the pontiff's passing late the *next* evening.

But this news lists the clerics that attended to the pope in his last hours, and Bishop Alphonsus de' Liguori is *on* that list and is reported to have been praying at the pope's bedside for several hours before his death. The Church's investigation on Alphonsus de' Liguori's supernatural experience of September 22nd uncovers dozens of eye witnesses. Those in Rome agree that he was there, praying and speaking to others, while those in Arezzo agree that he was in a trance in his Arezzo armchair. And Pope Clement XIV died in Rome on September 22, 1774, at seven o'clock in the morning, at the very time the ecstasy of Bishop Alphonsus came to an end.

Did the bishop bilocate to Rome or could he have traveled 270 round-trip miles between Arezzo and Rome in 24 hours? To answer this, let's presume that the bishop conducts a 6AM Mass on 9/21, then afterwards, slumps in his armchair and pretends to meditate. He then slips out the palace back door and at 7AM (sunrise in Arezzo that day), boards a horse-drawn *flying coach* service travelling 6-8 miles per hour with replacement horses all along the 135-mile route. Let's even assume he sets a new travel rate record of 10 miles per hour. With no breaks along the route, it would take 13 ½ hours to get to Rome by 8:30PM, with some of the resultant travel at night because of that day's 7:07PM sunset. If he spends 1½ hours with the pope instead of the stated *several hours*, he would board the return coach to Arezzo at about 10PM. He sets another *flying coach* travel record back to Arezzo, this time with a blistering rate of 15 miles per hour, all at night – and sneaks back into his room and into his armchair, just in time to ring the bell at 7AM to alert his staff of his desire to say another morning Mass.

Can a nearly 78-year-old man, with no telegraphic services, dupe his whole staff into thinking that he is slumped in a chair for a straight 24 hours, and also travel 270 miles by horse-drawn carriage at breakneck speeds in 24 hours? Only *bilocation* can explain this event.

Beach-sandaled monk arrives in snow, Flushing, NY, 1960

James Rummo was a boy living in Pietrelcina, Italy, around 1909–1916. He remembers delivering eggs from his grandmother's farm to Padre Pio, a Capuchin monk. Pio – who would later become a saint – was in his twenties and recuperating from poor health, so the eggs were delivered in the hopes of strengthening him. James' family was finding it difficult to find work in Pietrelcina, so they along with others moved to New York City. There the men joined the "Pietrelcina Society", which sent financial aid home to those who had stayed behind.

Years passed. James' daughter, Ellie Hunt, 31 years old, recalls an unusual event in 1960 after her grandfather, Jack Crafa, lapses into a coma at his Flushing, New York home. Ellie and her parents were at her grandfather's bedside when a stranger knocked at the door. It was a Capuchin Monk dressed in a dark brown habit. Ellie was surprised because there were no Capuchin Orders in the vicinity, and this monk, wearing sandals and no socks, was a misfit for the cold temperatures and the snowy conditions. He said he had come to pray for her grandfather. Since the parish priest had not arrived yet, the monk was an adequate proxy and so was invited in.

The young religious showed great kindness and compassion towards Ellie's grandfather, performing Last Rites and blessing the family before leaving. James, Ellie's father, observes that there was no car waiting for him outside. He watches the monk walk up the street and disappear into the darkness. James suddenly becomes pale and quite shaken. Ellie's mother, Lucy, asked him why. James replied, "Don't you know who that was? It was Padre Pio. He came in bilocation to give the Last Rites to your father. He looked exactly like I remember him [50 years ago] when I used to deliver eggs to him in Pietrelcina."

AD 1620–1631: 500 visits from a Spanish Lady in Blue to Jumanos Indian tribes in Southwest, USA

It's 1620 in the New World, called America. Pilgrims land at Plymouth Rock. But the Southwest portion of the land is Spanish Territory. That year in New Spain (now New Mexico), Jumanos Indians receive their first visit from a *Lady in Blue*.

That Lady is Mary of Ágreda, who lives in Ágreda, Spain. As a child, Mary was inspired to pray for the Indians in New Spain because their souls would be forever lost if they did not know Jesus Christ. So, in 1620, at age 18, her deep prayers for them reveal visions of the Indian's region (specifically New Mexico) and of their peoples' barbaric conditions and customs. This inspires her even more to pray and sacrifice for these souls who live across the ocean.

In one prayer session, she is led into a rapt ecstasy that transports her to a different place with the sensations of seeing the peoples, their lands, and feeling the warmer temperatures. She begins preaching in Spanish about Catholicism and the Indians respond to her in their native language; both parties mysteriously understand each other. Because they don't know her name, they call her "Lady in Blue". Returning from her trance, she finds herself still in Spain.

The bilocations to New Mexico continue. Sometimes Mary is tortured by the Indians and left for dead. She feels the pain, but she recovers and continues to visit, finally convincing them that she must be preaching the Truth. They begin to listen and practice the new Faith.

Over the next 11 years, the miracle repeats itself more than 500 times. Her bilocations to the New World save more souls. Bilocation is the answer to her childhood prayer to save New Spain's indigenous peoples.

Archbishop Zúñiga of Mexico hears a report of a young nun teaching the Indians. How can a young nun survive in the wilderness of New Mexico while male missionaries there are being attacked and killed by hostile tribes? The report to Zúñiga comes from Mary Ágreda's priest and confessor in Spain, Father Sebastian Marcilla, who contacted Archbishop Zúñiga to learn if Mary's reports of bilocations to the Indian territories were correct. The director of the missions in New Spain, Father Benavides, is asked to investigate.

One answer comes to Benavides in 1629 while sitting outside the Isleta Mission in New Mexico. Fifty Jumanos Indians arrive from a great distance, Titlas (Texas). They claim they were able to find the Isleta Mission because of the directions given to them by the Lady in Blue, and they wish to be baptized, to live as Christians. The Jumanos are shown a picture of an older nun in like dress from Mary of Ágreda's convent. The Indians say that the blue outfit is the same, but their Lady in Blue is young and beautiful, and she comes to us from the sky. The Indians also recall: "She had spoken, shouted and harangued them … and showed them a cross. The nations of the Colorado River shot her with arrows, leaving her for dead on two occasions. Reviving, she disappeared into the air. They did not know where her house and dwelling were. After a few days, she returned again and then many times after to preach to them." Two missionaries are sent back with the Indians. These men are surprised to find the Indians well instructed in the Faith. Who did this, since no missionaries have visited this area? The answer comes 11 years later.

Father Benavides finally finds the mysterious nun, Mary of Ágreda, not in America, but in Ágreda, Spain, in a convent. He questions her about New Mexico and the native tribes. She describes the tribal customs, the missionaries' faces in detail and their labors in the Southwest, the nature of the climate and more. He says, "She told me so many tales of this country, that I did not even remember them myself, and she brought them back to my mind." Father Benavides is convinced that Mary of Ágreda was directly teaching the Jumanos in New Mexico. In 1634, Pope Urban VIII orders him to write an account of his personal investigations.

Later, Mary's bilocations draw the attention of the Spanish Inquisition. If her claims are found to be false, she might die at the stake. She is interrogated twice by the Holy Office of the Inquisition in 1635 and 1649. She ultimately does not stand trial, due to her position as moral advisor to Spain's King Philip.

In 1690, a quarter of a century after Mary of Ágreda's death, a Tejas Indian chief in eastern Texas said to Damian Manzanet, a Franciscan missionary, "...in times past [the Tejas Indians] had been visited frequently by a very beautiful woman, who used to come down from the heights, dressed in blue garments, and they wished to be like that woman." Also, in 1690, during a visit by Jesuit Missionaries to Pima and Yuma Arizona, the Indians told them: "A beautiful white woman carrying a cross came to their lands. She was dressed in white, gray, and blue... She spoke to them, shouted, and harangued them... The tribes of the Rio Colorado shot her with arrows and twice left her for dead. But coming to life, she left by air."

Topic #12: Reading Hearts

This is the supernatural gift of knowing what's in a person's heart; what's in their conscience. The *Catholic Encyclopedia* lists 19 types of mystical phenomena like *apparitions*, *bodily incorruptibility*, and *stigmata* – only one among the 19 is exempt from the possibility of either diabolic activity or natural occult powers and that is the Reading of Hearts (sometimes called the Reading of Souls).

Some priests and mystics could read hearts. Here are three examples among many: Saint John Vianney (d. 1859), Saint Jacinta Marto (d. 1920), and Saint John Bosco (d. 1888).

Saint John Vianney: He is one of the most documented heart readers. He spent 16-18 hours a day hearing confessions, and people from France and abroad trekked to visit him and to go to him in Confession. Here's one of his many heart readings:

Lyons, France, 1853: a group of young men set out for Ars, France. All are good Christians, except an old man; an unbeliever. Regardless, he joins the group at Church at around 3 PM. At that very moment Father John Vianney, the *Curé* of Ars, comes out of the sacristy and enters the Church, kneels down, stands up and turns around. His eyes set upon one in the group from Lyons – he signals for one of them to come up. "It is *you* he wants," the young men tell the astonished unbeliever. Embarrassed, the old man walks up to Father Vianney. The young men all agree: "As for us, we were chuckling inwardly, for we understood that the bird had been caught." The Curé shakes the old man's hand, saying, "It is a long time since you were at confession?" The old man replies: "My good Curé, it is something like 30 years, I believe." "Thirty years, my friend?" says the Curé. "Just think. It is 33 years; you were then at such a place..." "You are right, M. le Curé," says the old man. "Ah, well, so we are going to confession now, are we not?" invites the Curé.

The old man could not refuse the one with such insight into his own heart – and his own life's timeline. He adds: "I at once experienced a sensation of indefinable comfort." The confession made a new man of him.

Saint Jacinta Marto: She was the youngest shepherd among the three at the supernatural events in Fatima, Portugal, in 1917, and is currently the youngest non-martyred saint in the Catholic Church. In 1920, the Virgin Mary visited Jacinta Marto as she lay dying at the orphanage of Our Lady of the Miracles, Lisbon, Portugal. The orphanage's Superior, Mother Godinho, recorded prophetic statements made by Jacinta, which all came true. Jacinta also had the gift of reading hearts. An example, according to Mother Godinho: Jacinta was listening to an excellent sermon by a priest of high standing and reputation. Jacinta, though, was unimpressed and turned to the nun with the grave prediction: "That priest will turn out badly, Mother, even though you would not think it now." Not long after this, the priest abandoned the cloth and lived in open scandal.

Saint John Bosco: He lived in Turin, Italy, in the 1800s, and devoted his life to helping street boys and juvenile delinquents – he called the young group "The Oratory". He also was a champion Confessor, spending hours listening to confessions, sometimes while his dinner lay cold on a table. He invited many into the confessional, "Come, and go to Confession and make your peace with God." You could not resist his pleasant, confident, bold style and his ability to read hearts and consciences; you were resigned to make a confession to him *in the box*. Here is what made John Bosco famous as a heart reader:

- A newcomer to the Oratory defied John Bosco to read his soul, and if he could, then he was welcome to publish its secrets. "Come here", said John, with a smile. He whispered in the boy's ear, then stopped to see his reaction, then whispered some more, and the newcomer got redder and redder. He then accused John Bosco of being his confessor earlier that day. The other boys affirmed that John Bosco had not left the Oratory at all that day.

- Passing by another boy, John Bosco asked him why he had not gone to Confession, since he needed it badly. "Why, I made it yesterday…to Father Piero", said the boy. "No, no…you made it badly…you did not tell him this", and John then preceded to tell the boy a sin he had been ashamed to admit in the confessional. The boy burst into tears.

- John Bosco was also aware of an *odor* in those who had any moral impurities. His ability to read hearts was so well-known that some penitents who lacked the courage to admit their wrongs would simply say to John, "Tell me my sins", and after hearing them, would nod in agreement. Sometimes the offer to list a penitent's sins came from John: "Will you tell me or shall I tell you?"

…if only we would pause at the end of *every* day to reflect and read our *own* heart – our path would then be better and straighter.

Topic #13: Levitation

Levitation is when a body rises into the air and remains suspended. It is an involuntary supernatural gift. Twenty-five people in the last 2,000 years have experienced it, from the 1st century AD to Catherine of Siena (14th century) and Padre Pio (20th century). Although levitation is highly inconceivable, one case alone tells otherwise: Joseph of Cupertino (17th century), the *Flying Friar.*

Cupertino was a clumsy, simple-minded man, despised by his companions; even his mother doubted his human value. But his humble, child-like mind had a supernatural appreciation for heavenly images: when they were in view, his mind would induce rapt ecstasy and then zero gravity, causing him to levitate. Simply put, when contemplating God in Mass, or viewing holy relics, Cupertino often began to fly. Here are the facts on his flights:

- In a 35-year period, 150 witnesses saw Cupertino levitate and have recorded sworn depositions on it. These witnesses were highly trustworthy individuals such as cardinals, craftsmen, princesses, princes, surgeons, bishops, and even Pope Urban VIII. Roman inquisitors considered Cupertino a potential threat because of his celebrity, so they put him on trial. Author Michael Grosso, in his 2015 book, *The Man Who Could Fly*, said the inquisitors, after trial, "could see this guy had no secret motives, he was completely humble, and he was embarrassed by his abilities."

- Diarist Arcangelo di Rosmi logged 70 incidents of Cupertino's levitations.

- The supreme Catholic authority on evidence of miracles, and an expert on fraud and paranormal behavior, Prosper Lambertini, (later Pope Benedict XIV), at first opposed Cupertino's canonization. Lambertini was a critically minded man, but eventually even he had to yield to the evidence presented. In his *De Servorum Dei Beatificatione*, he says: "…eye-witnesses of unchallenged integrity gave evidence of the famous upliftings from the ground and prolonged flights of the aforesaid Servant of God when rapt in ecstasy". The evidence must have been impressive.

- John Frederick, the Duke of Brunswick, saw Joseph Cupertino levitate twice and was so overwhelmed by the sight that, in 1651, he converted from Lutheranism to Roman Catholicism.

A note on those who levitated in the last 2,000 years: the majority were made saints, but *not* because they could fly. Rather, they were declared saints because they obeyed the 10 Commandments, were humble, and avoided the sin of *pride*. Their uncontrollable ability to levitate embarrassed them. Given a choice, only an ascension *after* death would have been flight enough for them.

Topic #14: Eucharist-only Survival for 13 Years – Portugal, 1942–1955

1918: Fourteen-year-old Alexandrina da Costa and her sister, Deolinda, are home when three men violently enter and attempt to sexually assault them. Alexandrina jumps from a 2nd-floor window to preserve her purity. The fall breaks her spine, and doctors fear that her paralysis will only get worse. For the next five years she drags herself to church to the amazement of parishioners. At age 20, she becomes completely bedridden for the rest of her life.

In 1942, Alexandrina prays to Jesus to make her a victim soul, that is, one that suffers in union with Him for the conversion of sinners. She then begins an absolute fast – no food, no water – only a consecrated Host, the Eucharist, for daily nourishment.

February-March, 1943: Another fast is happening elsewhere: Mahatma Gandhi concludes his 21-day food fast (his longest ever) to help stop communal riots, in Delhi, India. He does consume water because the body normally cannot survive without it for more than 12 days.

Spring, 1943: News of Alexandrina's fast spreads far and fast. Crowds visit her, asking her to pray for them. But some who visit her are suspicious and suspect that she is a fraud. So the archbishop asks medical experts to test Alexandrina's claimed Eucharist-only fast.

June 10, 1943: Alexandrina obeys the archbishop and concedes to having her total fast medically certified. She is taken via ambulance to Foce Del Duro hospital, in Oporto, Portugal, but prior to entry, her face is covered and she is transported into the hospital and into her room. The cover is removed and she finds herself surrounded by doctors and nurses. She is isolated in this room for a month and under constant observation, while only receiving Holy Communion – the Eucharist – once every day.

Dr. Enrico Gomes di Araujo, the lead physician, charges two nurses with watching all of Alexandrina's movements. They are both stationed at her bed. Dr. Araujo believes that Alexandrina is a fraud, and he is determined to prove it. He approaches the investigation in a harsh manner: the nurses are forbidden to ask Alexandrina any questions and when one nurse tries to comfort her sister, Deolinda, she is immediately dismissed and forbidden from entering Alexandrina's room again. The doctor also tells Alexandrina, "Miss, don't think that you have come here to fast.", and he instructs the staff to "...take away all the clocks so that the sick woman will be ignorant of the time." The doctor's demeanor is probably driven by this thought: how can a poor female with a disability be able to do something that no rich, white man could do? And if he does not discredit her, then it will be an embarrassment to the power structure in that society.

Dr. Araujo then tries to treat Alexandrina with a medication, but she refuses it. For five days the nurses check on her, thinking that she is close to death. They keep her isolated, convinced that she'll either ask for food or die of starvation.

Never for one moment is she left alone. A relay team of doctors and nurses continue strict surveillance. They offer her food and show her tasty morsels, but she refuses all of it. Dr. Araujo visits her several times a day, and makes some surprise visits at night, in hopes of discovering her secret food stash. He interrogates her and offers food to her, but she refuses to take it. After some weeks, the doctor permits Deolinda to visit, but forbids her to touch Alexandrina. Nurses perform rigorous checks of the bed sheets daily, looking for cached food. And all linens are frequently taken away and inspected.

July 20, 1943 (Day 40): Dr. Araujo ends the *observation* and prepares to discharge Alexandrina. Her absolute fast with absence of urine during the 40 days is confirmed. Dr. Araujo says to her, "In October, I will come to visit you at Balasar, not as a doctor-spy, but as a friend who esteems you." The nurse who assisted Alexandrina during the last 10 days of her fast is also convinced of her truthfulness and later visits Alexandrina in Balasar and greets her like a friend.

The official medical report issued and signed by Dr. Enrico Gomes di Araujo of the Royal Academy of Medicine, Madrid – a specialist in nervous diseases and arthritis – confirms Alexandrina da Costa as "scientifically inexplicable". The key sentence states: "It is absolutely certain that during forty days of being bedridden in [a] hospital, the sick woman did not eat or drink and we believe such phenomenon could have happened during the past months, perhaps the past 13 months leaving us perplexed."

In addition to the medical report, there is a certificate signed by two other doctors. It reads: "We the undersigned, Dr. C. A. di Lima, Professor of the Faculty of Medicine of Oporto and Dr. E. A. D. de Azevedo, doctor graduate of the same Faculty, testify that, having examined Alexandrina Maria da Costa, aged 39, born and resident at Balasar...have confirmed her paralysis...And we also testify that the bedridden woman, from 10 June to 20 July 1943 remained in the sector for infantile paralysis at the Hospital of Foce del Duro, under the direction of Dr. Araujo and under the day and night surveillance by impartial persons....Her abstinence from solids and liquids was absolute....We testify also that she retained her weight, and her temperature, breathing, blood pressure, pulse and blood were normal while her mental faculties were constant and lucid and she had not, during these forty days, any natural necessities."

"The examination of the blood, made three weeks after her arrival in the hospital, is attached to this certificate and from it one sees how, considering the aforesaid abstinence from solids and liquids, science naturally has no explanation. The laws of physiology and biochemistry cannot account for the survival of this sick woman for forty days of absolute fast in the hospital...As for the phenomena observed every Friday at about 3 p.m. (i.e., her ecstasies), we believe they belong to the mystical order...For the sake of the truth, we have prepared this certificate which we sign. Oporto, 26 July 1943."

Joao Marques, professor of medical science in Pernambuco and university lecturer of the faculty of medicine, examines Alexandrina's medical reports and the investigation's notes and then signs a report with the following testimony:

"In my opinion, it is not possible to explain by purely scientific means, or better still, by medical means, that which has happened to Alexandrina da Costa. Nothing makes us believe, according to what one reads in the detailed reports of the doctors and the confessor, that it is simply a matter of hysteria, particularly in view of the long time in which the sick woman has passed, and is still passing, without taking the slightest nourishment. On the other hand, I am certain that it is not a matter of deception because the impartial commission which observed her for forty days and forty nights with rigorous vigilance, could verify that her abstinence from nourishment was total."

"Now this abstinence from all food during such a long period of time is incompatible with life, and much less with the maintenance of normal temperature, respiration, pulse, blood pressure, etc... Her intellectual life is intense, her relationships are perfect, her faculties and senses are retained in an absolute manner...This extraordinary case, rather I would say exceptional case, can in no way be explained by purely natural means, or through scientific data. The inflammation of the spinal cord, which is most probably the cause of the paralysis, has nothing to do with her abstinence from food..."

There we have the verdict of medical science testifying to the truth of Alexandrina's fast. But Alexandrina has a more enlightened explanation. She confides to her confessor that Our Lord told her, "You are living by the Eucharist alone because I want to prove to the world the power of the Eucharist and the power of my life in souls."

Let it be known, too: Between 1942 and 1955, Alexandrina da Costa continued to live only on the Eucharist in her last 13 years of life!

A final look back: could she have cheated, and if so, why? She was, after all, in intense pain throughout her life, and she disliked the attention from the endless, visiting gawkers. Why cheat if the end result is unwanted attention – something very unpleasant to her – and, endure it all for *13 years*? Only a masochist or lunatic would do that – something Alexandrina was not, according to those who testified on her *fast*. They said that she was mentally competent.

Survival for 13 years without food or water? Bread can't do this! Nor this: Jesse Romero – former Los Angeles Deputy Sheriff, former Police Olympic boxing champion, and former USA middleweight kickboxing champion – has witnessed the effects of Jesus truly in the consecrated bread, also called the *Blessed Sacrament*. Mr. Romero was in the Los Angeles Sports Arena in 1983 with 20,000 Catholics when Jesus Christ was being presented in a monstrance by Father Juan Santillan. Father surprised the crowd by requesting that all gang-bangers, drug addicts, and porn addicts come down and lay before Jesus their weapons, drugs, and porn materials. How likely was this? Well, hundreds and hundreds came down from their seats in front of the arena crowd and they emptied their pockets and purses and dropped a collective, mountain-size pile of sin-and-vice paraphernalia before Christ. In a separate Catholic conference, Jesse's own mother – who days later was scheduled to undergo open-heart surgery – had her 90% blocked arteries healed by believing that Jesus was truly present in the Blessed Sacrament on display by Mexican priest and charismatic healer, Father Emiliano Tardiff. Doctors, who had seen Mrs. Romero's heart damage on several occasions, abruptly canceled her surgery because they now unexplainably found within her the arteries of a 30-year-old.

Jesus truly *is* in the consecrated Host. The Host is not just a bread wafer. These Blessed Sacrament miracles are done by Jesus Himself, through the Catholic priests – bread can't do this!

Humbly go visit Jesus – the God of the universe – in Eucharistic Adoration, and you will ***never*** be the same.

Topic #15: The Big Bang ➔ the *Effect* which begs a *Cause*

1929: Edwin Hubble discovers that the universe is expanding. This means that it was smaller in the past, so it might have a starting point.

1930s: The *Big Bang* theory bursts onto the world stage at a science conference. Georges Lemaître – a Catholic priest, astronomer and professor of physics – presents the theory as the *Hypothesis of the Primeval Atom*. Albert Einstein said of it: "This is the most beautiful and satisfactory explanation of creation to which I have ever listened." The theory describes the beginning of the universe as a singular point of extremely hot and dense matter that suddenly inflates faster than the speed of light, creating a mini universe. Space continues to expand for the next 13.8 billion years, "…carrying galaxies with it, like raisins in a rising loaf of bread." (Dr. Adam Reiss – paraphrased)

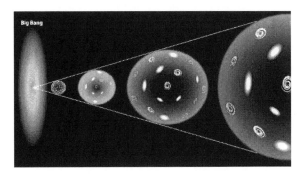

1959: One third of scientists believe in the Big Bang versus the *Steady State* theory, which describes a universe that has no beginning and no end. But the latter theory will meet its own end five years later.

1964: Arno Penzias and Robert Wilson discover a persistent, pervasive microwave signal in space. Their discovery confirms something in Lemaître's theory: The Cosmic Microwave Background (CMB) radiation. It is the first light rays, released just thousands of years *after* the initial big bang. The CMB temperature is taken in all of space and found to be uniform. Also uniform is the concentration of matter found in each large chunk of space. These observations both prove that all of CMB and matter itself came from the same region, that is to say, the same singular point, which again points to one Big Bang. The CMB discovery is the first evidence that the universe *has* a beginning – it results in Penzias and Wilson receiving the 1978 Nobel Prize.

2015: Einstein is right yet again. Scientists finally prove the existence of grav-itational waves first posited in his 1915 *General Theory of Relativity*. Scientists say that these waves also point to one Big Bang.

Today: Virtually all believe in the Big Bang theory. But it is the *Effect*; so, what is the *Cause*? Does *Nothingness* – a state devoid of all matter, intelligence, forces, liquids, gases – play a part here? No, the Big Bang is the EFFECT; it is a moment of creation caused by an agent outside of space and time – a great CAUSE➔ God. The director of the U.S. National Aeronautics and Space Ad-ministration's Goddard Institute for Space Studies in 1979 said, "…what came before the Big Bang is the most interesting question of all."

The discoveries in 1929, the 1930s, 1964 and 2015 are well-aligned with a state-ment made thousands of years ago: "In the beginning God created the heavens and the earth…Then God said, 'Let there be light'; and there was light." (Genesis 1:1)

Topic #16: The Universe's Fine-Tuned Physical Constants – Who monkeyed with them?

The fine-tuned physical *constants* are numerical values that were created one millionth of a second after the Big Bang and are critical to our Universe. The constants lie in a very narrow range, and if they were to stray out of that range, then matter, life and even the Universe would not exist. Here are just two examples, out of many:

- The Fine-Structure Constant, a, is a measure of how much mass is converted to energy when hydrogen atoms collide and fuse together. This fusion is how heat energy is produced by stars such as our Sun. The constant's value is 1/137 (roughly 0.007). If it were instead, 0.006, then stellar fusion would not produce carbon, which is vital for life. Further, if a had a value of 0.1 or greater, then fusion from stars would be impossible, so no place in the universe would be warm enough for life.
- The mass of a proton is a constant: 1.673×10^{-27} kilograms. Increase its mass by just 2 parts in 1,000 and all the universe's protons would then turn into neutrons.

Owen Gingerich, Professor Emeritus of Astronomy at Harvard University, gave a 2013 lecture at Gordon College, Massachusetts, relating the fine-tuned constants to the Big Bang: "The balance between the energy of expansion and the braking power of gravitation had to be extraordinarily exact." He explains: "Had the original energy of the Big Bang explosion been less, the universe would have fallen back in on itself (because of gravity) long before there was time to build the elements required for life. Had the energy been greater, it is quite likely that the density, and hence the gravitational pull, of matter would have diminished too swiftly for stars and galaxies to form." He says that the balance had to be accurate to 1 part in 10^{59}, which is 1 part in:

100,000,000,000,000,000,000,000,000,000,000,000,000,000,000,000,000,000,000,000.

The latter precision is far greater than this: successfully measuring by hand the distance from Earth to Pluto and being right to within the width of a human hair. This is supernatural precision, only achievable by an Intelligent Designer of the Universe – all for the benefit of humankind. *Chance* has no say here.

Some scientists, however, do not believe in an Intelligent Designer. They counter with one theoretical idea: the existence of a multiverse – a condition where millions and millions of universes exist, each with its own set of physical constants; ours being one with values that produce life. This *theory* is just that, since there is no proof of *any* other universe besides our own.

Back to reality: many scientists agree that the physical constants are remarkably fine-tuned. In his 1988 book, *A Brief History of Time*, physicist Stephen Hawking said: "The laws of science, as we know them at present, contain many fundamental numbers, like the size of the electric charge of the electron and the ratio of the masses of the proton and the electron…The remarkable fact is that the values of these numbers seem to have been very finely adjusted to make possible the development of life." In the 1981 *Engineering and Science* article, "The Universe: Past and Present Reflections", astronomer Sir Fred Hoyle, said, "A common sense interpretation of the facts suggests that a super intellect has monkeyed with physics." And, American theoretical physicist, Michio Kaku, once said, "If you change the mass of the proton, the charge on the electron, or any of an array of other constants, we'd all be dead." Finally, Dr. Benjamin Wiker conducted a 2007 interview with the world's most famous *atheist* of the late 20th century, Philosopher Antony Flew. Mr. Flew said that he became a believer in God because of "… my growing empathy with the insight of Einstein and other noted scientists that there had to be an Intelligence behind the integrated complexity of the physical Universe."

Topic #17: In an Egg Factory, what happens when you give a Twisted Ladder to a Butcher, Painter, Builder, and Welder?

We are all familiar with the twisted ladder, or DNA double helix that holds human biological codes and is the basis for creating a human being. But this can happen only if an egg cell divides, successor cells do likewise, and each cell has a copy of the DNA ladder. So, who replicates the ladder before cell division? That work is done by the butcher, painter, builder, and welder enzymes – the four biological machines at work in a human cell prior to its split. Follow the process text below in association with the diagram on the next page (a July, 2019, original art work by Mariana Ruiz Villarreal, AKA LadyofHats):

The butcher enzyme (Helicase) cuts the double helix ladder lengthwise through the middle of each rung. The painter enzyme (Primase) then primes each half ladder with acids to mark the starting point for the builder's task. The builder enzyme (Polymerase) creates more DNA rungs using only 4 rung types. The Welder enzyme (Ligase) seals any empty spots on the new structure. Once the new DNA is completed, the cell divides into two and now each cell has its own biologically-coded DNA double helix.

These four-enzyme teams continue their work in cells for 9 months until a human being emerges with about 37 trillion cells in about 200 different varieties along with 11 body systems such as skeletal, circulatory, reproductive, and nervous. This brand-new human being now has brain cells that it will use to fathom science, physics, music and math; learn a language; recognize danger and flee; hear, speak, see, and smell; play piano like Rachmaninov; and juggle while riding a unicycle.

STOP: Can anyone on Earth view (next-page) *human cell* DNA replication – done by tiny enzymes each somehow *programmed* to do a *different* job in *locked* step – and still say that this cell machinery was simply born by chance in Earth's chemical-soup mix? An *unceasing, designed process* over *coded* [DNA] matter within *all* cells – all by soup?

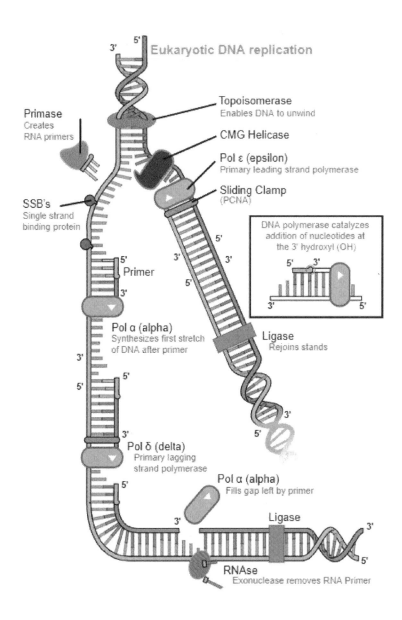

The enzyme story is just a tip-of-the-finger description of the whole process for making a human being. Here are some other questions to help convince you of the origin of human life:

1) How does a single cell become 37 trillion cells and how does this 1 cell become 200 types (e.g., heart cell, brain cell, skin cell)?

2) How did the first cell emerge with its own, inner organic machines, like *mitochondria*, to make energy for it?

3) How did a twisted ladder get embedded in a cell?

4) What tells a cell to divide?

5) What made the butcher/painter/builder/welder enzymes, and how did they learn *what* to do and *when*?

6) What mechanism ensures that a human being is always produced from a man and a woman's fertilized egg, instead of, say, an insect, a whale, or maybe a chimpanzee, whose DNA is 95% similar to humans?

7) How did the DNA ladder sequence its codes to only produce body parts in this order: head-to-neck-to torso-to legs-to feet?

8) DNA has codes for instincts like *fear, mating* and *rearing young*. And DNA has programming to create a reproductive system within each organism. Humans and animals would not exist without these two things. How did they get in the DNA?

9) DNA has codes that give each bird species a specific song or call to allow it to find a like mate. DNA also tells each species not to mate with other types. What are the causes of these things?

10) How did DNA create and embed these instincts into these organisms: sea turtles, newly hatched on a beach, will automatically move toward the ocean; a kangaroo climbs into its mother's pouch upon being born; honeybees communicate by dancing in the direction of a food source?

These are only a few of the many questions on the topic of life – a topic on which dogged research is required to arrive at valid conclusions. Scientists pursue answers in this way, so it's worth hearing what they have to say about the subject of life.

Sir Fred Hoyle, famous English astronomer and converted-atheist, said that he calculated the chance of obtaining the required set of enzymes for even the simplest living cell to be one in $10^{40,000}$ (one followed by 40,000 zeroes). Since the number of atoms in the known universe is infinitesimally tiny by comparison (10^{80}), even a whole universe full of primordial soup wouldn't have a chance. In his 1984 book, *The Intelligent Universe*, Hoyle also said, "Imagine 10^{50} blind persons each with a scrambled Rubik's cube, and try to conceive of the chance of them all simultaneously arriving at the solved form. You have a [like] chance…of [amino acids producing]… just one of the many [proteins] on which life depends. The notion that not only the [proteins] but the operating program of a living cell could be arrived at by chance in a primordial organic soup here on the Earth is evidently nonsense of a high order."

Philosopher Antony Flew, a nascent God-believer, said this: "The philosophical question that has not been answered in origin-of-life studies is this: How can a universe of mindless matter produce beings with intrinsic ends, self-replication capabilities [reproductive systems], and 'coded chemistry'? Here we are not dealing with biology, but an entirely different category of problem." Antony flew the atheist coop in 2004.

Final thoughts:

DNA is the blueprint for *you* and is contained in each of your cells. Each human cell has 3 billion DNA codes, so each is like a 3-billion-letter software program. DNA must then be the work of a supernatural Programmer. More evidence for a Divine Programmer lies in human beings' *capacity* to feel love and recognize truth, beauty and goodness. The latter capacities are evidence of a *soul* – a branding stamp placed on us by the Creator. This *branding* is done prior to the start of the enzymatic work in the first [fertilized] cell – when the four enzymes first pause… and wait…as God imparts the soul with words:

"Let Us make human beings in our image, after our likeness." [Genesis 1:26]

Topic #18: The Universe's Mathematical Equations

The Universe's math equations reveal *order* and *design*, not *Randomness*. On a grand scale, these equations rule the Universe – on a local level, they increase our happiness. The three equations below, for example, are important to rock climbers, foodies and travelers, can give us cheap energy or even a better social life. Their beauty lies in their simplicity, while their power lies in their usefulness. Life is good under these rules:

Pythagorean Theorem: $\qquad\qquad a^2 + b^2 = c^2$ (1)

Newton's 2nd Law of Motion: $\qquad\quad F = ma$ (2)

Einstein's Mass-Energy Equivalence: $\quad E = mc^2$ (3)

(1) Pythagorean Theorem (**PT**): In the *Wizard of Oz*, Scarecrow's new brain had its first thought: "The sum of the square roots of any two sides of an isosceles triangle is equal to the square root of the remaining side. Oh joy! Rapture! I got a brain!" (Technically, it's inaccurate. The sum of the squares of the two *smaller sides* of a right triangle is equal to the square of the *largest* side.) Nonetheless, this formula is plenty important to us. It's been used by everyone from painters on ladders to pizza men, and it's the talk of media experts, as well.

PT is always used in school with right triangles, but few know that it can be used on any topics that *are* or *behave* in 2 dimensions, like *the area of a shape*, or *sorting objects*, or *networks*. It's most useful in this general way:

Area(BIG) = Area(MEDIUM)+Area(SMALL)   **PT-Gen formula**

Practical, useful examples:
a) Pizza deals ➔ A shop offers for $10 either: one large 16" [diameter] pizza or two pizzas: one medium 12" and one small 10". Which deal do you choose? The two pies appear to be the better deal, but the total *area* of pizza in each choice is:

16" pie➔ 64 π square inches   (CHOICE 1)
12" pie (36π sq.in.)+10" pie(25π sq.in.)➔61π sq.in   (CHOICE 2)

64 π versus 61 π, so the better deal is buying the one large pie in CHOICE 1. But the owner saves almost 9.5 (3 π) square inches of

pizza ingredients (about 5%) every time a customer chooses the other deal. How's this deal related to the Pythagorean Theorem? Well, the owner knows that pizzas have *area* (with 16" pies having a radius of **8"**, 12" pies with radius **6"**, and 10" pies with radius **5"**). So, PT-Gen applies: $(8")^2 = (6")^2 + (?")^2$. The question mark is approximately 5.3, therefore, offering a smaller pie with radius 5" instead of 5.3 inches will result in a savings for the business. But now you, the foodie, know how to use PT-Gen as well.

b) A retired person needs a ramp built to access their home. The front stairs have a vertical height of 5 feet, and the ramp should begin 12 feet in front of the top step. How long must the ramp be? The Pythagorean Theorem is used to get the answer:

$$5^2 + 12^2 = RampLeg^2;$$
$$169 \quad = RampLeg^2;$$

Finally, 13 is the answer for the length of the ramp.

c) Metcalfe's network law says that given a network of size n, the value of it to a business is about n^2. Example: if a network grows to twice its original size, then its value is now 4 times greater to the business. The PT-Gen formula can be used to judge the value of certain sized social networks. A known right triangle is 5-12-13 (like in the previous Ramp problem), so we can use its numbers here to make a point:

Big Network = Medium Network + Small Network ➜
Network of 13 Million = Network of 12 Million+Network of 5 Million

The moral: A network of 13 Million is about as valuable to a business as the alternate scenario of being involved instead in two smaller networks with a collective total of 17 Million people. So, a business should focus on growing their presence on the largest network, and that growth, n, will display an n^2 increase in value to them.

(2) Newton's 2nd Law of Motion: F = ma, simply means "the more *Force* (F) applied, the more *acceleration* (a) will occur on an object of *mass* (m)". Think of pushing a car by yourself, then pushing it with a team of rugby players.

If you know Newton's 2nd law, then you know 90% of all applied physics, because this law is used for a staggering number of everyday cases and is a workhorse in science and engineering. It applies to all things in the Universe: apples falling from trees, baseballs flying into the outfield, the Earth orbiting the Sun. It helped get us to the Moon, and it applies to the motion of stars and galaxies, too. It also calculates:

- How much engine horsepower (Force) it will take to accelerate a train.
- Whether a plane will fly or not.
- How air currents move: misjudging these forces led to the 1940 Tacoma Narrows Bridge disaster.
- Whether a cannon ball will reach its target.
- How many people can safely ride in an elevator with a known acceleration.
- How strong a Pike's Peak, Colorado, guardrail must be in order to stop a vehicle of a certain mass from careening through it and over the cliff.
- The existing forces on all bridge materials to know whether a bridge might collapse.
- The force exerted on umbrella fabric by metal spokes accelerating at a rate needed to arrest the rain. Umbrellas with protruding spokes show a failed application of this law.

Finally, this law calculates the maximum force allowed on a small, closed loop, called a carabiner that accepts and secures a rope. The strength of the small but mighty carabiner is a lifesaver to a tethered, 200-pound rock climber accidentally free-falling at $9.8 \ meters/second^2$.

F = ma ➔ an elegant formula that mitigates universal force calculations.

(3) Einstein's Mass-Energy Equation: $E = mc^2$ ➔ An equation where *energy* (E) equals *mass* (m) times the *speed of light* (c) squared. And c is 186,000 miles per second, akin to 7.5 trips around Earth per second.

The equation says that energy and mass (i.e., matter) are essentially the same thing. Put another way: matter contains a whole lot of energy. In fact, the website emc2-explained.info states, "Each atom of a substance can be thought of as a little ball of tightly packed energy that can be released under certain circumstances", and in Einstein's own words, "...very small amounts of mass may be converted into a very large amount of energy..."

Two atomic processes obey $E = mc^2$ and output huge amounts of energy:

- Fission energy: this occurs when an atom is split. Fission energy is produced in nuclear power plants. Emc2-explained.info says, "This energy is about a *million times* more energy than is released by the burning of one molecule of petrol (gas) in a car's engine…if you currently use a tank of petrol each week but could use the energy provided by one tank of uranium-235 fission instead, you wouldn't need to refill your car for over 19,000 years." While fission doesn't produce carbon pollutants as does wood, coal, gas, and oil burning, it does produce radioactive waste that can last for 1,000 years, and its power plants can leak radiation, like in the actual 1986 Chernobyl disaster, in the now-abandoned town of Pripyat, Russia.

- Fusion energy: It occurs when 2 atoms fuse together, with energy as output. It is the process which powers the Sun, whose energy travels to Earth in 8.5 minutes, arriving as light and heat.

This form of energy is the choice among all because:
  o Fusion, per particle, releases about 7 times more energy than fission.
  o Sea water is its (abundant) fuel supply, and only a postage stamp weight's-worth is used at a time.
  o It requires only about three buckets of seawater a day to satisfy the world's daily energy needs.
  o Helium is its main waste product. (Birthday parties will benefit.)
  o It's safe: reactor meltdowns don't occur; reactions just stop.
  o *Bonus*: Fusion plasma – prior to its use for electrical production – may be used to incinerate garbage and solid wastes. The incineration will also produce raw materials for industry.

But if fusion energy production is the ultimate process, then why not do fusion *now*? Because the process requires a temperature about six times hotter than the Sun's core. Still, scientists are making progress on creating sustainable fusion reactions and the world is investing billions of dollars to make fusion energy production a reality by 2050. If it is achieved by then, at its root is the conversion of mass into energy through equation: $E = mc^2$.

These are just three of the simple, useful, and well-designed mathematical equations that rule our Universe. And when the dream energy called *Fusion* becomes reality, then we'll finally be out of Kansas and in the Land of Oz.

Topic #19: The Conscience and the Soul – Two great gifts for our happiness, now and forever

The **conscience** is the moral law *written on our hearts*, kind of like a virtuous Global Positioning System (GPS). It knows what is right and good. When you are faced with a moral choice, the conscience provides you with direction; if you ignore it, you feel guilty. But beware: if you continue to ignore your conscience, it will become weaker and more distant, until you lose your way in life.

Proof of a conscience exists. Careful studies and experiments were done at Yale University by Professors of Psychology, Karen Wynn, and Paul Bloom – reported in May 2010, *New York Times Magazine* – show that we are born with a rudimentary sense of justice. "There are hard-wired moral universals [in our DNA]," says Professor Bloom. "At birth, babies are endowed with compassion, with empathy, with the beginnings of a sense of fairness."

Our conscience initially seems to be a nag, attempting to deny our body and mind certain pleasures – expecting us to practice self-control and sacrifice. But, if we follow it regularly, we come to realize that the conscience maximizes our happiness and contributes to others' happiness, too.

The *soul* is a spiritual entity, separate from the body. It is the *essence* of a human being.

The soul is our ticket to life after death and happiness forever *if* in our lifetime we have obeyed our moral GPS. But does the soul really exist? To answer this, we need to examine two worlds:

- Material world: The *mind* interacts with the material world through the five senses. The mind receives input, mixes in potential memories stored in the brain, and then makes a decision. The mind's main role is to keep the body alive by satisfying its desires and needs.
- Immaterial world: The immaterial world consists of the great ideas, like Love, Goodness, Truth and Beauty. What prods us to pursue these in order to make us a better version of ourself? Further, what causes us to yearn for justice, freedom, and equality of opportunity for all? And what reminds us to avoid becoming a slave to gluttony, greed, envy, anger, pride, lust, and laziness? It's the soul.

All great ideas go beyond the mind. They belong to the *soul*, our inner essence, that which prods us to improve our *character*.

The soul motivates us to shed bad habits and embrace good ones. Its driving mantra is this 3rd century quote:

"Watch your thoughts, they become words –
watch your words, they become actions –
watch your actions, they become habits –
watch your habits, they become character –
watch your character, for it becomes your destiny." – Lao Tzu

There is no better proof of the existence of the soul than when it sees vulnerable people in danger. While the mind thinks, "Don't go there", or "Don't do that", the soul says, "But I must... because it is the right thing to do". The soul, here, reveals itself as the agent of courage.

Courage is the result of *love* – a willing act of sacrifice or suffering for others' sake. Here are three examples of souls in action:

- Private First Class (PFC), Desmond T. Doss, a conscientious objector and medic in WWII, saved many lives on Hacksaw Ridge in the Battle of Okinawa in 1945. His Citation states: "...As our troops gained the [Hacksaw] summit, a heavy concentration of artillery, mortar and machinegun fire crashed into them, inflicting approximately 75 casualties and driving the others back. PFC Doss refused to seek cover and remained in the fire-swept area with the many stricken, carrying them one by one to the edge of the escarpment and there lowering them on a rope-supported litter [stretcher] down the face of a cliff to friendly hands. On 2 May, he exposed himself to heavy rifle and mortar fire in rescuing a wounded man 200 yards forward of the lines on the same escarpment; and two days later he treated four men who had been cut down while assaulting a strongly defended cave, advancing through a shower of grenades to within eight yards of enemy forces in a cave's mouth, where he dressed his comrades' wounds before making four separate trips under fire to evacuate them to safety. On 5 May, he unhesitatingly braved enemy shelling and small arms fire to assist an artillery officer. He applied bandages, moved his patient to a spot that offered protection from small-arms fire and, while artillery and mortar shells fell close by, [he] painstakingly administered plasma. Later that day, when an American was severely wounded by fire from a cave, PFC Doss crawled to him where he had fallen 25 feet from the enemy position, rendered aid, and carried him 100 yards to safety while continually exposed to enemy fire. On 21 May, in a night attack on high ground near Shuri, he remained in exposed territory while the rest of his company took cover, fearlessly risking the chance that he would be mistaken for [the combatant] and giving aid to the injured until he was himself seriously wounded in the legs by the explosion of a grenade. Rather than call another aid man from cover, he cared for his own injuries and waited five hours before litter bearers reached him and started carrying him to cover. The trio was caught in an enemy tank attack and PFC Doss, seeing a more critically wounded man nearby, crawled off the litter and directed the bearers to give their first attention to the other man. Awaiting the litter bearers' return, he was again struck, this time suffering a compound fracture of one arm. With magnificent fortitude he bound a rifle stock to his shattered arm as a splint and then crawled 300 yards over rough terrain to the aid station. Through his outstanding bravery and unflinching determination in the face of desperately dangerous conditions PFC Doss saved the lives of many soldiers. His name became a symbol…for outstanding gallantry far above and beyond the call of duty."

- In 1986, Unit 4 of Chernobyl's nuclear power plant was destroyed, spewing massive amounts of radioactive material into the environment. The immediate death toll was possibly in the thousands and would later include the plant's firefighters who unknowingly would lose their lives to radiation poisoning.

During the disaster, a molten radioactive material was created and began flowing towards a huge pool of water lying under the reactor. If the flow reached the pool, it might have set off steam explosions that would destroy the other three Chernobyl reactors, firing radiation high and wide into the sky, spreading across parts of Europe, Asia, and Africa. "Our experts studied the possibility and concluded that the explosion would have had a force of three to five megatons," said Soviet physicist Vassili Nesterenko. "Minsk, which is 320 kilometers from Chernobyl, would have been razed and Europe rendered uninhabitable."

This water pool had to be drained! Someone was needed to wade through radioactive waters to reach the underwater drain valve. Three men, Alexei Ananenko, Valeri Bezpalov, and Boris Baranov, were chosen and suited up in scuba gear to do the job. They stepped into the darkness beneath a molten radioactive flow and put the good of humanity before their own safety. They found the valves and drained the pool.

But more trouble loomed: the molten flow might penetrate Unit 4's concrete floor, seeping into the Black Sea and contaminating the water supply of millions. A group of 400 miners were asked to work in extreme levels of radiation to build a tunnel under the concrete to prevent the poisoning of the Black Sea. In the six weeks that it took to complete the tunnel, the miners were exposed to radiation levels equivalent to between 80,000 and 160,000 chest X-rays. The human damage was done. In the years ahead, about 100 miners of the 400 would die before they reached age 40. Miner Vladimir Naumov reflected years later on the Chernobyl digging: "Who else but us? Me and my fellow workers were brought up that way. Not that we went there to die, we went there to save lives…to save our families first and our country, of course."

The noble sacrifice of all these men greatly reduced the deaths within Europe and Asia for years to come.

- In 2007, Malala Yousafzai was 10 years old when the Taliban took control of her region: Swat Valley, Pakistan. The Taliban banned girls from attending school and destroyed some 400 schools. Malala had a firm belief in her right to be educated, so she stood up to them. "How dare the Taliban take away my basic right to education?" she once said on Pakistani TV. In 2009, and over the next three years, Malala's voice grew louder and she and her father became known throughout Pakistan for their determination to educate Pakistani girls. But this angered the Taliban and resulted in their shooting of 15-year-old Malala Yousafzai on October 9, 2012. She survived and was moved to Birmingham, England, for multiple surgeries, including one to fix the paralyzed left side of her face. After recovery and therapy, she continued her education in Birmingham.

This story of a strong, defiant teenage girl, who was shot and almost killed, would usually end here with her physical and educational needs being met in a "safe zone". But Malala had other plans:

- o On her 16th birthday in 2013, Malala visited New York and spoke at the United Nations about her desire for education for every child, especially girls and also for children of the extremists, especially the Taliban.
- o Later that year, she published a book entitled, *I Am Malala: The Girl Who Stood Up for Education and Was Shot by the Taliban.*

- o In 2014, Malala traveled to Jordan to meet Syrian refugees, and to Kenya to meet female students.
- o That same year in Nigeria, she spoke out in support of the abducted girls who were kidnapped earlier that year by Boko Haram, a terrorist group which, like the Taliban, tried to stop girls from going to school.
- o In October 2014, Malala was named a Nobel Peace Prize winner. At 17 years old, she was the youngest person ever to receive this prize.

Desmond Doss, the Chernobyl firefighters, Alexei Ananenko, Valeri Bezpalov, Boris Baranov, the 400 miners, and Malala Yousafzai: In their minds they knew the danger and may have first thought, "Stop…too risky…turn back". But each one's soul sensed a human need, compelling them to ignore the risks and push through the danger.

Near-death experiences also support the notion of a soul. Charlotte Martial, researcher at the University Hospital of Liège, in Belgium, analyzed 154 written accounts of near-death experiences. The most common shared experiences were a feeling of peacefulness (reported in 80 percent of the accounts), seeing a bright light (69 percent), and encountering with spirits or people (64 percent). One third of participants (35 percent) began their episode with an out-of-body experience and ended with a return to the body (36 percent). "This suggests that near-death experiences seem to be regularly triggered by a sense of detachment from the physical body and end when returning to one's body," Martial said.

Finally, evidence of a soul and of humans as spiritual beings is contained in written accounts thousands of years old:

- [As seen in the three stories above] "…the spirit is alive because of righteousness." [Romans 8:10]
- "And He [Jesus] said to him, 'You shall love the Lord your God with all your heart and with all your soul and with all your mind.'" [Matthew 22:37]
- "Before I formed you in the womb I knew you…" [Jeremiah 1:5]

Every human has a soul, which means we're destined for a supernatural end. The salvation or loss of a soul is the most profound meditation of existence.

Topic #20: Human Consciousness: How does this immaterial thing control the material world?

Science cannot answer this question. It is a mystery that causes even deep-thinking atheists to pause and ponder God.

The human mind is the source of consciousness. Could a mind capable of logic, language, creativity, math calculations, and emotions be created by a haphazard mixing together of atoms and proteins over millions of years? *Think* about this.

Consciousness has no physical presence in the world. Images and thoughts have no measurable dimensions. So how does the mind direct the brain to move our bodies?

The mind uses the brain to process more than 100,000 messages per second. Its activity is so vast that it takes a circa 2014 supercomputer about 40 minutes to map one second of brain activity. This extremely powerful, dimensionless, immaterial entity called human consciousness is what has driven science and advancements in the past few thousand years.

The human mind also conceived and created *material* products like lasers and lights, TVs and telephones, satellites and space ships, computers, cars and airplanes; further proof of its supernatural properties – and more evidence for the existence of a supernatural God.

Finally, Sir Nevill Francis Mott, winner of the 1977 Nobel Prize for Physics, said this: "Neither physical science nor psychology can ever 'explain' human consciousness. To me then, human consciousness lies outside of science, and it is here that I seek the relationship between God and man."

Topic #21: Unique faces, fingerprints, footprints and DNA: designs for a safer and happier life

"That's not fair!" What child hasn't exclaimed this (once or a million times) to their parents, playmates or coach. The innate yearning for justice and fairness is unique to humans, just like each human face is unique. Just imagine if human faces were *not* unique. What might that do to a sense of fairness?

- You could be wrongly accused of a murder.
- You could approach a stranger you thought was your friend. Awkward!
- An angry person might confuse you for his enemy.
- Your virtual twin might claim a reward meant for you.
- This "twin" might also go into the local bank and withdraw money from your account
- You might be given the wrong drugs at the local pharmacy.
- A look-alike stranger could enter your house and get overly acquainted with your spouse.

But we are unique – even identical twins, in a subtle way. Unique faces, among 7.5 billion people (and among the 100 billion people who have ever lived) virtually eliminate all the above scenarios resulting in a safer and happier existence.

Did you know that fingerprints are 10 times more unique than human faces? They are unique for every person, among identical siblings, and even for each of your 10 fingers. There are currently 66 million fingerprints in the U.S. national database, including those of government employees, military personnel and, of course, criminals. Used for the first time in 1892 to solve a crime, fingerprint *match* queries can be satisfied within 10 minutes.

Is it just a coincidence that finger tips are unique? Who is responsible for this feature?

Toe prints are also unique and have been used to nab barefoot bandits, like in the 1952 robbery of a Scottish bakery with a flour-dusted floor, and in the 2010 Washington State capture of an international robber who left his pedal mark in a grocery store.

And what of crimes perpetrated by savvy glove-wearing or shod individuals? There's always DNA in saliva, blood, hair – any of which could easily be deposited at a crime scene. DNA testing began around 1986. More recent advances in DNA analysis boast the ability to distinguish between identical twins

– so even they have lost their get-out-of-jail-free cards. DNA can also determine if people are related or whether an organism caused a disease. So, DNA is a blessing because it helps us identify and possibly remove evil and disease from our midst.

In addition to DNA, there are 11 unique human identifiers in all: the iris, ear, lip print, tongue, voice, finger and toe print, teeth, retina, hair, and gait. Let's take a closer look at three.

- The ear appears to be even more secure than fingerprints, since the latter could be worn down. The ear is fully formed at birth, with only a slight descent over time. Ear prints have been found to be 99% accurate and can be useful for secure, computer recognition.
- The iris (a muscle that controls the opening and closing of the pupil based on the intensity of light) is unique even for identical siblings, and even unique between each of your own two eyes.
- Foot pressure patterns during a normal human gait allow researchers to uniquely identify a person 99% of the time.

We have, thus far, discussed many unique, ordered, and coded human characteristics. This *order* and *code* point to a Designer. If, instead, humans are the work of *Nothingness* or *Randomness,* then what are the odds this would result in 100 billion unique faces, DNA, and all the other 11 unique human identifiers?

Topic #22: Christianity – *born* in two supernatural events, *sustained* in martyrs' blood, *thriving* by having something to die for.

Christianity was born around AD 33 in Jerusalem where Judaism was the religion and Romans ruled. Its teachings and proclamations of Jesus as God and of the Resurrection were misaligned with Judaism and also not in accordance with the Romans' belief in other gods. This new religion, born in alien soil, should never have survived.

Christianity was put to the test by a Judaic zealot named Saul of Tarsus, who tried to extinguish it. In AD 36 after witnessing the death of Stephen, the first Christian martyr, Saul and several companions traveled 136 miles to pursue the execution of Christians in Damascus. While they made their way along a sunlit road, a bright light appeared. Saul was struck blind. He heard a voice say, "Saul, Saul, why are you persecuting me?...I am Jesus, whom you are persecuting." (Acts 9:4-5) His companions also heard the voice. Saul was guided to Damascus where he did not eat or drink for three days. He miraculously regained his eyesight and converted to Christianity. The conversion of a Christian-hunter, Saul, into the Christian apostle Paul – alone – proves that Christianity occurred through Divine Revelation. Paul's conversion also proves that Jesus Christ rose from the dead. Nothing but the power of a supernatural event could change a religious extremist's heart, mind, and belief system. Further proof that *Paul encountered Jesu*s – the second supernatural event – is evident in Paul's 25 years of suffering and service in the name of Christianity:

- Paul was stoned in Lystra, dragged out of the city and left for dead. He courageously returned to continue preaching the Gospel.
- He was rod-whipped three times by the Romans and rope-whipped five separate times by the Jews.
- Paul was shipwrecked three times and once floated in the deep for an entire day.
- He was in constant peril of robbers.
- Paul was likely beheaded in Rome in the AD 60s for the crimes of preaching the Gospel of Jesus Christ. But not before completing a ride through life like no other, which culminated in his inspired writings which comprise about 25 percent of the New Testament and his conversion of thousands to Christianity over 10,000 traveled miles.

Christianity grew because of the evangelization efforts of Paul, the 11 original apostles and other disciples. But Romans ruled the region and launched sporadic attacks against Christianity in the first 300 years. Roman Emperor, Nero, for example, in AD 64, falsely pinned the Great Fire of Rome on the Christians. For why not blame a group that refused to pay homage to Roman gods, and were considered cannibals – claiming to eat the flesh and blood of their leader? Roman historian, Tacitus – after the great fire – wrote *this* on the Christian persecutions:

"In their very deaths they [the Christians] were made the subjects of sport: for they were covered with the hides of wild beasts, and worried to death by dogs, or nailed to crosses, or set fire to, and when the day waned, burned to serve for the evening lights….For this cause a feeling of compassion arose [among Roman citizens] towards the sufferers…because they seemed not to be cut off for the public good, but were victims of the ferocity of one man."

Early Christian theologian, Tertullian, said, "The blood of martyrs is the seed of the [Christian] church." Martyrs helped sustain the early Christians and were considered by tens of thousands of people as a spiritual 'height' to aspire to and imitate. Roman citizens lacking purpose and direction began to think that Christians had some powerful reason for which to live *and* to die: in the arena; on the cross; being stoned; or beheaded. For it was their faith in Jesus – the risen God – that allowed Christians to choose a shameful, agonizing public death *over* being reinstated as a full Roman citizen simply by sprinkling some incense over a Roman god altar as a sign of respect.

The martyrs had an incredible effect on people's imaginations because they gave witness to something of value and had the answer to the question: what is your life worth if you don't have something to die for?

Some martyrs among many were:

- Peter – the first Christian pope – who was crucified in AD 67 by the Roman emperor, Nero.
- 28 of the first 31 popes.
- At least 3 direct apostles of Jesus killed by crucifixion, stabbing by sword or spear, or stoned.
- Vibia Perpetua, a young mother in Carthage, North Africa, in AD 203, became a new convert to Christianity when it was against Roman law. She proclaimed her new faith and was therefore sentenced to death in the Roman theatre – to be gored by a wild bull. She willingly went to her death. Her prison diary and three eyewitnesses described her suffering and trials up to the day of her martyrdom.

- Lorenzo Ruiz (of Chinese-Filipino descent) was a 17th-century Catholic missionary, church clerk, and married father of three living in Manila, Philippines. In 1636, he was falsely accused of murder, so he left Manila and sought asylum on board a ship bound for Japan. A storm forced the boat aground near Okinawa, in a region ruled by anti-Catholics. Lorenzo and other missionaries were caught and given a choice: abandon your Faith and be freed, or be tortured. They wouldn't abandon Christ, so they were bodily tortured for a year by being crushed, stabbed, soaked, pressed and cut. Finally, refusing one last time to deny Catholicism, Lorenzo and some others were executed this way: they were hung upside-down over a pit and their heads were cut to allow blood collecting there to bleed out, preventing them from losing consciousness and to prolong their agony. Lorenzo Ruiz died from blood loss and suffocation. He was a true Catholic martyr and became the first Filipino saint when he was canonized in 1987 by Pope John Paul II.
- In 2015, 20 Coptic Christians were killed by ISIL. A non-Christian was amongst them, but when the terrorists asked him if he rejected Jesus, he said, "Their God is my God." He was then martyred, too.

Converts to Christianity were also inspired by the efforts of non-martyred Christians, who served others through the creation and administration of primitive hospitals, education centers, and houses for poor widows and orphans. Roman citizens took notice of Christians' austere morals, humility, clear purpose, and firm stand against Roman society's practice of infanticide. For example, if a newborn came at an inconvenient time, was disfigured, was the second girl, or was a financial burden, some Roman fathers would choose to *expose* the baby, leaving it out in the open to die in the cold, be eaten by animals or, perhaps more humanely, would be taken by someone to be their servant or slave. Christians would pick up the baby and raise it as their own, baptizing it, and using community funds to raise it. Over time, the Christian way of conquering human hearts overwhelmed the Roman Empire. The last pagan Roman Emperor, Julian, who reigned from AD 361-363, clearly understood the power of the Christian way when he wrote: "These impious Galileans (Christians) not only feed their own, but ours also…" He also recognized that the Roman Empire would not succumb to enemies of the State, but rather to love, the love of Christ. Julian's dying words in AD 363 were "Vicisti, Galilaee" (You have won, Galilean [Christian]).

So how did Christianity, without army or weapons and its leader killed – survive, grow and sustain itself through persecutions to become over 2 billion members strong today:

- Proclaiming its leader as a God-man born to a human mother among animals in a stable?
- Claiming that its leader grew up in a poor carpenter's family, later hob-knobbed with sinners, prostitutes and tax collectors and then willingly, like a lamb, laid down His life to save *them* for all eternity?
- Insisting that its leader rose from the dead!?

And how could this Christianity cause people to reform their lives, put themselves on the line for the sake of the good of the other, and join a Church which brought them hostility, estrangement from family members and neighbors, and likely persecution to the point of death?

Those are super long odds; so long that they could only be covered by Divine interactions and the promise of Paradise to those who are in a state of grace and perform earthly acts of love towards God and others. These acts simply overwhelmed the Roman Empire and resulted in Christianity becoming its official religion in AD 380. The growth of Christianity over centuries is also proof of its truth.

St. Paul's message to the living just prior to his likely death by beheading is the great message of hope that also helped motivate people to embrace Christianity: "For I am already being poured out like a libation, and the time of my departure is at hand. I have competed well; I have finished the race; I have kept the faith. From now on the crown of righteousness awaits me, which the Lord, the just Judge, will award to me on that day; and not only to me, *but to all who have longed for His appearance.*" [2 Timothy 4:6-8; italics added]

Topic #23: Dying ➜ proof that our home is elsewhere

No one escapes death. Among the billions of people who have ever lived, not even one born in the late 1800s is still alive.

One hundred billion is the estimated number of people who have ever lived. If the universe has no God, and *Chance* or *Randomness* is responsible for its being, then the odds that one person would have escaped death is virtually 100%. Yet zero people out of 100 billion have escaped it. This proves that the process of *Dying* is designed, and designed so well that it has zero defects. That makes *Dying* a supernatural process.

Where's the evidence of *design* in dying? It's at the human cell level:

- The human cell nucleus contains twisted ladder strands – our Deoxyribo-nucleic acid (DNA) – which identifies **us** as us. This DNA is within each of our chromosomes. At the tips of the chromosomes are telomeres, which act like caps, similar to the caps at the end of our shoelaces. Telomeres keep our chromosomes' DNA ends from fraying and protect the inner DNA – our identity – from being lost during cell division. But with each successive round of DNA replication, the telomere tips get smaller and smaller – like a lit bomb fuse over time – as a cell progresses through 50-70 cell divisions. The telomere ends eventually shrink to nothing, which halts a cell's divisions and leads to their death. This shortening of the telomere tips is associated with aging, cancer, a higher risk of death, and potentially linked to Alzheimer's disease, hardening of the arteries, high blood pressure, and type-2 diabetes. The dying design here: A *consistent, specific range* of cell divisions occur before telomeres – the cell's timekeepers – are shaved to nothing leading to an eventual cell death. The range is 50-70 divisions.
- Cell death also includes the carefully planned out, programmed process, called *apoptosis*. It occurs, for example, in skin and hair cells.
- Aging is most likely a result of stress on cells caused by oxidation – where the oxidants are produced through normal breathing.
- Aging, too, is most likely caused by glycation, where glucose sugar – normally eaten for energy – binds to some of our DNA, proteins, and lipids, leaving them unable to do their jobs.

So, the *dying* process has, or most likely includes:

- a natural, cellular, telomere-shortening process that eventually causes a cell's natural death
- the breathing of oxygenated air
- the eating of sugar for energy

And dying as a normal part of life is stated in ancient writings:

- Genesis 3:19: [God to first man, Adam] "By the sweat of your brow you shall eat bread, until you return to the ground, from which you were taken; for you are dust, and to dust you shall return."
- John 14:2-3: [Jesus speaking to His apostles at the Last Supper, prior to His own death for our sakes] "In my Father's house there are many dwelling places. If there were not, would I have told you that I am going to prepare a place for you? And if I go and prepare a place for you, I will come back again and take you to myself, so that where I am you also may be."

Dying proves that our real home is elsewhere: in a place being prepared by God for all who believe, are baptized, and do good.

Topic #24: Earth ➜ Created to support life by design or happenchance?

There are reasons why Earth can support life:

- It orbits at an optimum distance from a heat source – any closer or further away would be catastrophic to life.
- It is home to a substance that *flows* and *scatters* – one vital for flowing nutrients to plants, animals, and internal human organs. Water accumulates by evaporation and clings to clouds for transport across the entire planet to drop as rain for the benefit of all living things.
- Earth has *gravity* to keep all matter in place; else we're just dust in the wind.
- Earth is the *right size* to produce enough gravity and retain an atmosphere with life-giving gases like oxygen and nitrogen. Too much gravity would cause harmful, lighter-than-air gases, like ammonia and methane, to linger near the ground. Too little gravity would allow oxygen and nitrogen to leak out into space. Mars, which is only half the size of the earth, lost most of its atmosphere due to too little gravity and lack of a magnetic field.
- Earth's spherical shape is the result of gravity pushing all matter towards its center. Earth *must rotate* to ensure that its entire surface has moderate temperatures. The daily sunrise is proof that Earth does rotate. Standing still or rotating more slowly would cause extreme surface temperatures, like those of Venus, which has a dark side temperature of -283°F – cold enough for carbon-dioxide-snow – and a sunny side temperature of 860°F.
- Earth has the Moon, an orbiting rock just the right size to stabilize Earth's axis, thereby moderating its weather. The Moon's gravitational pull maintains Earth's rotation at an optimal speed to quell extreme winds and temperature.
- The Earth's source of light and heat – the Sun – also emits deadly solar radiation. Earth just happens to be equipped with a magnetic *force field* that protects it and funnels most of the harmful radiation towards its two poles. There the solar radiation collides with oxygen atoms to produce greenish yellow and red lights and nitrogen atoms to produce blue light – the phenomenon commonly known as the Northern and Southern Lights.
- BONUS: With the existing magnetic field, we can use a compass to navigate the planet. The magnetic field also is used as a Global Positioning System (GPS) by about 50 animal species, ranging from birds and mammals to reptiles and insects. For example, tiny amounts of iron in the neurons of a

bird's inner ear align with Earth's magnetic field for accurate north-south migrations. What creates this magnetic field? The Earth's ample rotation causes its hot, liquid iron core to flow and produce electric currents that in turn create the magnetic field. So, the Earth acts like an engine – a generator – that produces electromagnetic energy.

The Earth's Sun/Moon relationship. What a coincidence.

- From Earth, the Sun and Moon appear the same size because although the sun is almost 400 times larger than the Moon, it is also nearly 400 times further away. So, the apparent same-size Sun and Moon is the cause of total solar eclipses where the Moon disc almost perfectly matches and covers the Sun disc. What are the odds that the number *400* would occur in both size and distance relationships between two objects?

Further, do scientists have a handle on the origins of Earth's properties? No. Here are their uncertain thoughts on just two:

- *Planet rotation*: Scientists say this: "As an interstellar cloud collapses, it fragments into smaller pieces, each collapsing independently and each carrying part of the original angular momentum. The rotating clouds flatten into protostellar disks, out of which individual stars and their planets form. **By a mechanism not fully understood** but believed to be associated with the strong magnetic fields associated with a young star, most of the angular momentum is transferred into the remnant accretion disk."
- *Gravity*: Scientists say: "So, what is gravity and where does it come from? To be honest, **we're not entirely sure**." Sir Isaac Newton even had to conclude that gravity amongst the planets in a solar system could not naturally be explained, so "It is the will of God."

What are the odds that Earth would be in constant orbit around a heat source; be the right size to create the right amount of *gravity* to ground all living matter and to sustain an atmosphere; have a sidekick Moon of just the right size to stabilize Earth's axis for bearable weather and winds; *rotate* at the right speed and with the aid of the Moon to moderate winds and temperatures; have a protective force field with a built-in GPS? And what are the odds that the number *400* would occur in both size and distance relationships between the Sun and the Moon?

Can this three-way relationship among the Earth, Moon, and Sun be dumb-luck or something else? You decide.

Topic #25: Earth's pharmacy is hiring…

Wanted: Hobos/food artists/medicinal chemists for work in a 57 million square mile pharmacy. Travel, via land, air, or water, required. Must possess the skill to design foods that look like the human body parts they benefit and be able to make medicines to treat human ailments or diseases. Finally, you must be incapable of reasoning. Inquire within Earth.

What fits this job description better than *plants*? For they are:

- Hobos – and the world's best. By land, they spread their seeds through colorful, sweet fruit that entices birds and mammals to take a bite and deposit the undigested seed elsewhere. By air, they send their spores or pollen to germinate same-species plants. By sea, plants, like cranberries, have air chambers that allow them to float and disperse seeds via water. This "hobo" scatter strategy ensures the survival of the plants.
- Food artists: Did you know there are plant foods that are *preventative medicine* for similarly shaped human body parts. Take the walnut. It looks like a brain, protects brain health in newborns and improves cognitive performance in adults.
- Medicinal chemists: Over 17,000 plant species produce *reactive* medicines – those which treat existing ailments and diseases. Medicines, for example, may be extracted from these plants:
  - Madagascar Island's Rosy Periwinkle plant has medicinal qualities that increase the odds of surviving childhood leukemia from 10% to 95%.
  - Papaya fruit has properties that help shrink disks in the human spine.
  - The Cinchona tree's quinine is used to treat mosquito-borne malaria.
  - Chili peppers include a capsaicin compound that alleviates the pain of arthritis and shingles.
  - The yarrow root is helpful for toothaches.

Plants, these seemingly mindless wonders, have for centuries *manipulated* birds and mammals into spreading their seeds all over the Earth, launched their grains into the air like *flying gigolos* in search of a mate, and instinctively *shaped* themselves like the human organs they benefit. Then, with unsolicited *compassion*, they help to formulate medicines to heal human beings.

But how? By the plant's Deoxyribonucleic Acid (DNA) and its double helix structure, with its ordered pairs of four possible chemical building blocks. This internal 'software' programming determines these things:

- Plant type: annual, perennial, biennial, groundcover, evergreen, deciduous, aquatic, vine, bulb, shrub, grass, rush, sedge, cactus, succulent, or tropical
- Shape and size
- Whether it has seeds, spores, pollen, or flowers
- What chemical compounds it produces

DNA is the currency in Earth's pharmacy. DNA reveals a supernatural, planned and ordered foundation for humanity; part of a love story that even extends to foods resembling the parts they benefit as in the images below.

Coincidence or design? What say you?

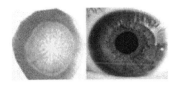

A carrot's layers are like those in the human eye's iris. Carrots contain beta-carotene, which is converted into Vitamin A, an important nutrient for the eye. Vitamin A deficiency can easily lead to eye dryness, swollen eyelids, or even blindness.

Grapes resemble the alveoli – the smaller airways of the lungs. These lung structures allow oxygen to pass from lungs to the blood stream. An ample diet of fresh grapes has been shown to reduce the risk of lung cancer and emphysema.

Ginger root (left) resembles the human stomach. Ginger contains gingerols and shogaols, which help treat upset stomachs, and relieve motion sickness nausea.

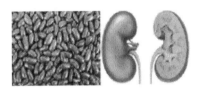

Kidney beans (left) are shaped very much like human kidneys (right) and also provide minerals and vitamins to heal and maintain kidney function. **Caution:** you might need to moderate your intake of kidney beans if your kidneys are diseased.

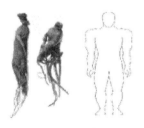

Ginseng root looks like a human body and it potentially is a holistic cure for many ailments, including fatigue, stress, diabetes, and insomnia. The Mayo Clinic found that ginseng improved fatigue in cancer patients after 8 weeks.

Caution: side effects can occur if you eat too much ginseng or eat a poor-quality root.

An avocado resembles a baby in the womb. Vitamin E in avocados helps balance hormones, shed off baby weight, and prevent cervical cancer. Its folate also helps prevent birth defects.

The pancreas (right) is part of the digestive system, and sweet potatoes (left) not only look like it but also help in the production of insulin by the pancreas. This helps balance the glycemic index of diabetics.

Beefsteak tomatoes & hearts have chambers. Tomatoes have lycopene, an antioxidant which helps to reduce the risk of heart disease & some cancers. Tomatoes have potassium – good for patients with high blood pressure – and Vitamin B6, which neutralizes 1 chemical that causes damage to blood vessel walls.

Walnuts (underlying) look like a brain (top). Walnuts are full of omega-3s, which help to keep the brain fluid and flexible. Walnuts can also prevent you from becoming depressed and can boost your mental well-being.

The tiny green tips on a broccoli head (left) resemble a clump of cancer cells (right). The US National Cancer Institute discovered that weekly servings of broccoli were enough to reduce the risk of prostate cancer by 45%.

Onions (left) look like the body's cells (right), and they clear waste materials from them. The chromium in onions regulates blood sugar. And the quercetin compound in onions plays a significant role in preventing the formation of cancer cells.

A digested banana creates the brain's mood chemical: serotonin. So, a banana is like an anti-depressant drug: eating one will cheer you up and put a smile on your face.

➔Caution: Eating too much of any beneficial food could lead to toxicity – be careful◀

Question 1: Does God Exist? →

The Answer: Part 1 of 3

Compelling evidence for God's existence was presented in the topics above. More will be given later to fully answer the question: *Does God exist?* Let's first review some of the topical evidence:

- Apostles willingly go to their deaths by preaching about the resurrected Jesus. Would they have endured this fate if this were a lie? Would you go to your death over a lie?

- Three young shepherds claim visits from the Virgin Mary. The town's authority drags each off to be boiled in oil unless they tell the truth. They never change their story. In Mary's visit in July 1917, she tells the children that a miracle will happen midday, October 13th, *and it does*, in front of 70,000 people.

- AD 1530s: eight million Aztecs convert to Catholicism (3,000/day) based on the indestructible, photo-like, cactus-cloth image of the Virgin Mary that has a constant human temperature and which caused a Japanese ophthalmologist to faint, claiming the image's eyes were alive and looking at him.

- At Lourdes, a young French girl's hand is immersed in flame for 15 minutes without harm to her while she is in ecstasy listening to the Virgin Mary. At least 69 miracles occur because of the waters at this sacred site.

- A Host turns to heart flesh, and wine to blood globules. Both remain alive and fresh after 1,200 years. To those who say of the consecrated Host, "It looks and tastes like a wafer, so it must be a wafer, not truly Jesus", consider the same reality you place on a quarter dollar. "It's hard, so it must be solid metal". In fact, it's 99.9999% empty space! (It feels hard because your fingers are pushing on the metal atoms' outer-shell electrons, not on the atoms' nuclei.) Each atom is virtually empty space, so why does your sense of touch say otherwise? It's time to re-think your disbelief concerning the consecrated Host.

- 100 trillion bacteria live in us and assist with decomposition after death, underground, in an 8-50-years' time span. But nearly 250 devout Roman Catholics' bodies have not decomposed in hundreds of years. How do bacteria choose to spare some from decomposition, and only Roman Catholics?

- AD 1914-1921: 2,500 sworn testimonies are given on the true facial expressions, body movements, sweating, bleeding and frothing from Jesus on the cross that resides in a church in Spain.
- Bilocation is a special gift where an individual can be in two places at once. In AD 1620-1631, how did a Spanish nun visit southwest, USA, and its native Indians, 500 times while still seen in her convent in Spain?
- Joseph of Cupertino was viewed flying on many occasions by 150 witnesses who submitted sworn depositions on the events. The Duke of Brunswick, seeing Joseph of Cupertino levitate twice, was so overwhelmed by the sight that he quickly converted from Lutheranism to Roman Catholicism.
- A Catholic woman lives for 40 days in a hospital without food or water, taking in only the Eucharist.
- Atheist writer and philosopher, Antony Flew, shocks the world by suddenly becoming a believer in God because of "…my growing empathy with the insight of Einstein and other noted scientists that there had to be an Intelligence behind the integrated complexity of the physical Universe."
- A human fertilized egg cell becomes about 37 trillion cells, comprised of 200 cell types and 11 body systems (e.g., skeletal, reproductive, and nervous). The four biological cell machines – doing different jobs in ordered steps – produce an exact copy of DNA prior to any cell's division to create human life. Where did these biological machines get the smarts to do their work? And, if *Randomness* is responsible for creating humans, then what are the odds that the first human emerges *with* a reproductive system?
- Science cannot explain how physical atoms and molecules create human *consciousness*. Consciousness is comprised of images and thoughts with no measurable dimensions, but somehow it crosses over to then direct our brain to move our body. Sir Neville Francis Mott, winner of the 1977 Nobel Prize for Physics, says, "To me then, consciousness lies outside of science."
- Great designs exist for safety and security: we all have unique faces, fingerprints, footprints, and DNA.
- A supernatural event is the only explanation for the complete conversion of a religious zealot – Saul of Tarsus – *to* the Christian religion that he had been furiously persecuting. How else?
- How did Christianity survive with a small band of apostles without army or weapons and its leader just killed, preaching in hostile Roman Empire territory about the need to live a sacrificial life? And how did it thrive to become a Church with 2 billion+ members? It had to have supernatural help.

- Earth orbits a heat source, is the right size to produce adequate gravity to sustain an atmosphere, has a moon the right size to regulate Earth's rotation to help aid good weather and winds, has a magnetic field to help birds and us navigate the planet, and has a force field to protect it from the sun's harmful rays. Just happenchance? Ponder this too: what causes gravity?

These comprise an avalanche of evidence *for* a supernatural God. Caveat: The Catholic Church does not require that you believe in all this evidence. But it's presented here with the hopes that it might increase your faith in God.

Read on for more evidence for God's existence.

The Answer: Part 2 of 3

Additional Topics ➜ God versus Nothingness and the 'Gassy Ocean'/ Primordial Soup theories

God: Let's suppose He *does* exist. He, then, is the Designer and Creator of the universe. God first creates mathematics as the rules for the universe, then He produces the *material world* of things like atoms (with their proton and neutron combinations and placement of electrons in different orbitals giving them an orderly arrangement and predictable properties within all materials), space, light, sun, planets, gravity, earth, moon, water, land, sky, animals, birds, and fishes. All are in the *predictable* world (yes, even animals, birds, and fishes have set instincts). But what of the *unpredictable* world? God designed it, too: human life.

Here are the crucial blueprint questions for creating unpredictable and non-robotic human life. Should God:

1. Give humans freedom to think and act...or should He prohibit free will?
2. Give humans a perfect nature where *all* choices and behaviors are good... or an imperfect one?
3. Make human pleasure experiences cumulative...or fleeting?
4. Reveal Himself to every human being...or not?

Answers to questions 1 and 2 are easy. God's creation *must* include a free will and an imperfect nature, else humans would be like robots, *predictable* and the opposite of God's plan for human life.

To answer 3: If pleasures were cumulative, virtually all of us would become pleasure addicts over time – this again leads to robotic behavior. Fortunately, God has dialed down normal pleasure experiences to *fleeting*.

Note! ➔ These three designs are absolute: all humans with a healthy brain are free to think; all are imperfect and have sinned (except the Virgin Mary); and human pleasures are fleeting. Absoluteness that affects billions of people never exists by chance, but through a Designer.

The answer to question 4 requires some thought. Suppose God came down from Heaven, put His arm around each person, and said: "Hi, I'm God. Let's visit for one minute that which is yours after your life is over: Heaven. It's a place with no pain, no sorrows, no hunger, and no dangers. In 60 seconds, I'll set you back on Earth." Once back on Earth, each person would be like a robot, obeying God in all things, because they would intensely desire their revealed, eternal prize. But this God-in-your-face design is what good-natured Atheists ('God doesn't exist') and Agnostics ('unsure if God exists') want as proof of God, else they refuse to believe in Him. They are simply unaware that God-in-your-face is a *poor design*, and shoddy things are impossible for Him. So, their wish is *never* going to come true because He has a better idea:

Veil-and-Seek: Create a universe exhibiting design, code, beauty and order as evidence that 'God must be here', but veil from view the Deity as a mystery to compel humans to seek God – through faith.

If you were creating life, wouldn't you want your creation seeking you? Veil-and-Seek: another great idea!

Nothingness/Gassy Ocean/Primordial Soup:

Let's suppose God does *not* exist. That means the universe was created by *Nothingness*; by chance. So, the Earth was either a primordial soup – where life arises from non-living matter – or, an ocean with its floor gases combining to create primitive cells. But how confident are we that *Nothingness*, or a gassy ocean or hot soup, manufactured virtually everything:

- *Gravity:* Every object existing in space or on solid ground (from atoms to humans) has a gravitational pull on other objects. So, there are zero defects in the design of gravity. How was gravity created and made to be so consistent and true?

- Human *consciousness* came into existence and it learned how to control our bodies. How did it come to be and learn how to exist in both immaterial and material worlds?
- *Ideas* like Truth, Goodness, Love: could these immaterial things come from soup or ocean flatulence?
- *Beauty*: Where did it come from with its properties of *color* and *landscapes* as in the next image? (See the full-color image on the book's back cover)

And in its elegant mathematical rules shown here?

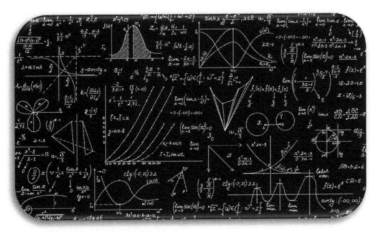

Music: Where in the universe did it come from? Dispersed in air, of human minds… played by the brain but reaching the heart and even touching the soul through works such as Barber's *Adagio*, Rachmaninov's Piano *Concerto #2, 2nd Movement*, or Bach's *Erbarme dich, mein Gott* (St. Matthew's Passion) – the latter work, by its ethereal nature, actually converted three atheists/agnostics to God believers (told by them to a famous author).

As for human life: are we on Earth by soup or gas – if not by God? Let's consider Mozart. Skilled on keyboard and violin at age five, he composed symphonies at age eight, and wrote a full opera at age 12. Or Alma Elizabeth Deutscher. Born 2005, she started playing piano at age two, composed at age four and wrote a full opera at age 10. (At age three she heard a Richard Strauss lullaby, and said, "…how can music be so beautiful?") Are these geniuses created by chemicals or by an infinitely more beautiful Source? The *beautiful Source* is much more believable given the fact that scientists have conducted many chemical experiments over half a century and have failed to produce a single evolutionary change of species.

So, what are the *odds* that universal things exhibiting design, code, beauty or order are *not* from God? Look below.

The Answer: Part 3 of 3
The 25 chapter topics are just a smattering of the world's miraculous events. For example, only three of the Virgin Mary apparitions were presented here, but in fact, there have been at least 16 deemed *worthy of belief* – out of 2,000 claimed visits. (The Catholic Church has a strict vetting process, approving less than 1% of Marian apparitions). Likewise, only three topics on Eucharistic miracles were presented out of 140 approved by the Vatican. This chapter could have included at least 175 topics. But, let us remain skeptical even between vetted-and-approved Marian apparitions and Eucharistic miracles. Let us count only *half* of all the approved topics. We then arrive at 97 topics that could have been discussed in this chapter: 8 Marian topics + 70 Eucharistic miracles + 19 of the 25 chapter topics = 97.

Now let's calculate the odds of debunking 97 supernatural topics. If all are debunked, then God is imaginary like the Tooth Fairy. Let's assign a generous 50% chance that each *will* eventually be declassified as *natural* – even though science has already picked over these topics for years. The generous odds, therefore, of debunking *all* 97 topics are these: $1 \div 2^{97}$, or about 1 in 16000000000000000000000000000000.

To understand these microscopic odds, we need to play a game with the 10,000 dots in the entire black box on this page. A computer chooses one dot among them, and then to win (akin to successfully debunking all 97 topics), you must guess what dot was chosen – not just in one game – in seven games in a row! Similarly, if the game were modified to mimic the odds of declassifying *all* 25 topics, then one dot is randomly chosen among 5,776 dots within the inner dashed box. To win, you have to correctly guess the randomly chosen dot in two games in a row – still a formidable task.

97-topic
Game➔ Choose one dot from 10,000 anywhere in the black box. Must win 7 games in a row.

25-topic
Game➔ Choose one dot from 5,776 anywhere in inner gray box. Must win 2 games in a row.

What are the odds? ➜

These supernatural topics cannot all be debunked. So, God *not* existing is as crazy an idea as "…the chance that a tornado sweeping through a junkyard might assemble a Boeing 747 from the materials therein." (Sir Fred Hoyle) God lives. Seek Him!

…Still don't see the *value* in believing in God through faith, then please consider these points.

Skier/Beachgoer view of eternity, and the *Eternity Game Wager*

Do you prefer a snow or sand vacation? Whichever…close your eyes and go to a snowy mountain or a vast, sandy beach. Now pick up a handful of snow or sand and blow it out of your hand until one snowflake or sand grain remains. In your hand is the duration of your brief life, compared to *eternity*: the entire mass of snowflakes or sand grains on the mountain or beach.

…Take a moment to grasp the difference between the one symbolic life in hand, and the eternal life out there…

Now, would you prefer a life's journey of purpose, sacrifice, and love of God and neighbor (a pilgrim's existence), or one favoring *your* wants and needs (a tourist's life)? With the answer in mind, play the Eternity Game:

ETERNITY GAME: WAGER ➜➜	If GOD exists…	If GOD doesn't exist…
I truly believe in God, so I live like a PILGRIM	♥ Humankind benefits from my life + Eternal reward for me	Humankind benefits from my life
I don't believe in God, so I live more like a TOURIST	*I mainly benefit from my life* + Eternal penalty for me	*I mainly benefit from my life*

The *heart* box is the best outcome. But some people reject this wager, with comments like:

1. "This wager is an offensive threat."
2. "This wager is nonsensical because you don't know what God to believe in."

Regarding #1: If the wager at least compels you to think about how your (short) life can benefit others, and after death, yourself; and you also come to live more like a pilgrim after grasping the infinite time difference between your life and eternity in the mountain/beach analogies, then this wager is a *good* threat.

Regarding #2: Among all religious people in the world, two out of every three believe in the God of Abraham. Among religions with an actual founder, then it's four out of every five people who believe in the God of Abraham. In Christianity, Jesus Christ is the second person in the Holy Trinity *within* the God of Abraham – one God, three Persons.

Jesus as God actually came to Earth to live, die, and resurrect for His creatures. Jesus' teachings are also perfect, so follow Him. Chapter 3 will cover, among many things, Jesus' Word, His commandments to us, and how to imitate Jesus in order to gain eternal life.

→ FINAL WORDS on Question #1

Human beings are built for happiness. We yearn for it and have in us a happiness void that must be filled. We try to fill it in two ways:

- As a TOURIST with an eat-drink-and-be-merry motivation.
- As a PILGRIM through challenging, purposeful events that subsequently produce happiness.

Pleasure is fleeting for everyone, so pleasurable events only fill the happiness void *during* the event. But when the event ends, the hole empties and a search begins for the next pleasurable event. This cycle continues throughout a TOURIST's short life until death. And the happiness void is never filled.

A PILGRIM discovers enduring happiness *after* challenging or sacrificial events, such as hard study to improve one's skills; exercise for improved energy; and volunteering to aid a neighbor. These events are not always pleasant, but the *results* are: knowing you're on the right path, making good decisions, living with purpose and improving the world through charity towards others. These are what fill the void and create a cumulative happiness.

The Shore of Belief: We have sailed through this chapter and have landed. We are now equipped to join one of two expeditions searching for the *cause* of the universe. Each team's causal evidence is given below:

God Team: Supernatural events, absolute/unwavering design for human life, consciousness, gravity, music, and math; ideas like truth, goodness, and love; programming, order and beauty all across the universe.

Non-God Team: Nothingness, Randomness, Chance, primordial soup, gassy oceans.

What say you on your choice of expedition? Remember: *life* and *pleasures* are fleeting like the wind, while eternity is **FOREVER**.

Wager your belief on a sure thing.

Question #2: Why am I here on Earth?

For those still unsure if God exists, then the last chapter spoke only to your *mind*. You're a person who also needs to *feel* God's existence. That does require you to travel the longest distance in the human body: from *head* to *heart*. But if you conquer this distance, then your heart will be moved to action – to seek and find God. Be assured, He is waiting for you!

For those who believe in God, the answer to why you're here on Earth is symbolized in this story:

AD 1895 – Cook Islands, Polynesia: You and a friend go fishing with a Māori fisherman guide on his small boat. A sudden storm arrives midday and drives the boat off-course towards a familiar five-square-mile island. But trying to land the boat in rough waters drives it onto a rocky ledge, severely damaging it and causing all to go overboard. Fortunately, everyone makes it to shore. You're okay, but the fisherman's leg has a large, bloody gash and your friend is dazed. The storm passes and the weather finally clears. But you're stranded here:

The **fisherman guide** – unable to walk – says this about the beautiful island:

"It's infested with coconut crabs that are armor-plated, can climb trees and are up to three feet long. They eat meat and can smell blood." However, he knows of a **buried chest** with survival supplies. He begins to give you a mental **map** to it just as you spot a few crabs heading your way.

He hopes that you are listening with **_great attentiveness_**: "To find the box, first walk the narrow path up to the top of the rise, then walk until you find a double-trunked palm tree. It's there where you will cross over a fast-moving brook. Then make a sharp right and walk about 500 feet through a palm grove and shimmy down the steep hill till it levels. The box is buried under the third-largest boulder...go quickly!"

Decision time: You can't take both men with you and you have no weapons and no place to hide from tree-climbing, **_armor-plated crabs_**. So, you choose your friend, hoist him on your back, and **_carry him_** up the rise. You drop him off at the top and journey alone. With instructions in mind, you run to find the treasure...

You have listened well and have found the survival box – filled with a machete, medicines, plant seeds, and canned fruits and vegetables. You grab the machete and head back to the shore, but the native fisherman is now dead among a swarm of coconut crabs. You kill about a dozen of them, and then you and your friend in the next couple days hunt and kill the rest. The island is now safe for habitation. To survive, you eat the local coconuts and fruits and slowly consume the canned foods. The island has fresh water, and you plant the seeds to start a garden. You're both resigned to life on this **_beautiful island_** for all time.

You remark to your friend how different life would be if you hadn't listened to the fisherman's words about the path to the treasure box. For without its survival gear, your remaining days would be an **_island hell_** – filled with sleepless nights as nocturnal, three-foot crabs hunt you for _their_ food.

The End.

The story's symbolic keys are:

- **fisherman guide:** the fisher-of-man – a wise Man with knowledge of a treasure that all should seek
- **buried chest:** the end prize for you and others
- **map:** the path...the Word – that must be followed to reach and obtain the prize
- **great attentiveness:** the degree to which you follow the Word to the treasure
- **armor-plated crabs:** ones coming to kill the bleeding guide; just like Roman soldiers crucified our Guide in AD 33

- **injured companion:** you help another on the steep and narrow path toward the prize
- **beautiful island:** a symbol of a good, long life – like an eternity with peace, joy, and beauty
- **island hell:** a symbol of a bad existence – like an eternity with stress, pain, and evil creatures

The story's moral:

God wants you to be happy forever, with Him. So, He sent you a living map to follow: Jesus. *You* choose your destiny based on *your* attentiveness to His Word. Your level of attentiveness will determine whether you inherit a quadrillion-grain sunny beach or a quicksand pit. Again, your choice. For something this crucial, shouldn't your *attentiveness* to Christ be as vital as the *blood of your heart?*

If you're reading this because you're convinced of God's existence, then you must also believe in His written map, the Bible. It consists of inspired writings. It contains two statements that describe life-or-death choices – both found at your Fork of Destiny.

Which **3:16** Bible verse will you choose to follow?

Fork of Destiny

Revelation 3:16 Path ➔ [God said] "So, because you are lukewarm, neither hot nor cold, I will spit you out of my mouth." Meaning? Lukewarm people will be separated from God. Not having time for God or being tempted by earthly riches and pleasures contributes to a lukewarm Faith. Most people are unaware that they're on this path because they're consumed by worldly things.

C.S. Lewis' *Screwtape Letters* describe this path well with a story of a senior devil, Screwtape, mentoring a junior devil, Wormwood, on how to tempt a Christian. Screwtape tells Wormwood, "...the safest road to hell is the gradual one...", and further, he tells him in a letter (with a 21st century twist) to keep up the [distractive] noise in Christians' lives:

"Cue the ambulance and the vibrating smart phone and erect the Victoria Secrets...billboards in the most conspicuous places where they'll draw attention and, with luck, cause the most accidents. Make their heads spin, their eyes dart, and their minds work overtime. As much as possible, create more traffic jams and road rage. Even in times of silence, flash a new thought every few seconds across their distracted, undisciplined minds. We have made great gains in recent years, but there is still so much we can do.

Now if necessary, you may even need to exploit some of the Enemy's (Screwtape's word for God) tools to achieve our ends. Use good causes to keep their schedules jam-packed. Remember: even good music and the occasional good TV show drown-out silence just as the bad ones do.

Remember: Do not grow weary in creating noise, sowing confusion, and promoting random acts of selfishness...

Your despicable uncle,

Screwtape"

John 3:16 Path ➔ "For God so loved the world that he gave his only Son, so that everyone who *believes* in Him might not perish but might have eternal life." Those who truly believe in God give of their time, talents, and treasure to God and others. They also do two things:

1. They heed God's law – written on their heart – by engaging and listening to their *Conscience*. The Yale University studies on human morality show that Conscience is hardwired in us before birth.
2. They practice *love of neighbor*, and through it, experience lasting joy. For altruism has been shown to activate the same pleasure parts of the brain stimulated by food and sex. This result has been verified by scientific, Magnetic Resonance Imaging (MRI). So, altruism is hardwired within us, too.

So now your soul is at the Fork:

➤ The God of the universe wants you to seek Him and be happy and be with Him forever. He offers you the gift of Heaven but expects you to choose it or not based on your free will. Jesus gave us advice on how to accept the Prize: "Love the Lord your God with all your heart, soul, and mind" and, "Love your neighbor as yourself." This summarizes Mark 16:16 ("Whoever believes and is baptized will be saved..."), the right-side Path. *Take it!*

➤ Satan, the devil – not a god but a puny, fallen angel – is allowed to tempt you. Satan hates God. He wants you at the end of your life to leave the gift of Heaven on the table. So, he throws distractions, busyness, and temptations in your path. All are calculated to stop you from practicing morality and love of neighbor. Satan knows that if he can run out your life clock before you morally progress and accept God's gift to you by living a modest and holy life then he has deprived God of your soul. He's also working hard to distract your loved ones, too. He has many people currently heading down the darkened, left-side Path, towards his web. *Avoid it!* There, he can prey upon you forever – just like a spider that snares, immobilizes and cocoons its prey.

Do you have the will to go *right*? The John 3:16 path is further fleshed out by St. Paul: "I have competed well; I have finished the race; I have kept the faith." [2 Tim. 4:7]. What does the latter mean to you and your eternal journey? What does it mean to be *in the race*?

The answer is in Aesop's *Hare and the Tortoise* fable ➜

The tortoise has *faith* because it believes in the finish line reward; it is *humble* because it knows that it has inferior speed to that of the hare, so it must *depend* on course directions to avoid getting lost and losing time; it has *hope* that it will keep running because it has *patience* with itself through its humility and firm commitment to the goal. Even though the tortoise was not born to go fast, it won't stop. It will *persevere* until the end.

For you to be *in the race* means to be like the tortoise ➜ Have *faith* that your race through the 8 streets will end in Jesus waiting to welcome you at the finish line; be *humble* in your pursuit of Heaven by *depending* on God in the Holy Spirit as your internal GPS to keep you on the straight path and on Jesus being always by your side; sustain *hope* by being *patient* with yourself even though you may morally fail; and exhibit *patience* when confronted with others' failures; for patience with others is *love*. *In-the-race* means that you try to always be in a state-of-grace (in a relationship with God, with no serious sins on your soul); try to stay pure in your thoughts, words, and deeds; **persevere** in heeding Jesus' teachings until life's end. Slow and steady wins this race to Paradise.

Good readers: Be alert! The degree to which you follow Jesus' Word in this short life sprint – with faith, humility, patience, love, and perseverance – determines your eternity. *Your Ending.* And a well-run foot race means that you crossed the finish line with absolutely nothing left to give – otherwise, you didn't try your best. Your earthly sprint begins at the moment of *Belief* and is not a fun-run or walk-in-the-woods. You don't win the eternal prize just by:

- Going to Sunday Mass
- Treating Jesus' Church's precepts like a menu: following only those which make sense and feel right to you
- Being holier than Hitler, Stalin, and Mao; or others you know.

Instead, you must persevere in a lifetime of carrying the tree of life – your cross – denying yourself and bringing the Kingdom of God to wherever you go.

Finally, the *answer* to this chapter's question is infinitely more important than all your other earthly goals and dreams:

Why am I here on Earth?

→ To help myself and others get to Heaven ←

You are helping yourself, but God is helping you, too. Your goal also aligns with this: "The things of this world, no matter how flashy, will all pass away. What matters is where we spend eternity." – Rich Donnelly, Major League Baseball coach

The last chapter will give you Jesus' map to Heaven. It's in yet another Bible verse 16: **Mark 16:16**: "Whoever believes and is baptized will be saved..."

Now, is this task of denying self and helping others too hard to bear? If yes, then you're like those in Jesus' time, who said: "Then who can be saved?" [Luke 18:26-27] Jesus replied, "The things that are impossible with people are possible with God." Translation: God is saying that you can't earn Heaven – rather, it's a **free gift**. But with anything given to you, you must **accept it**. An example: If God gives you the gift of certain skills, *accepting those* means you *use* them for good; else, it's like getting a wrapped present that you never unwrap and that you leave on the table at life's end. So, how do you accept the offering of Paradise? Follow the Mark 16:16 map detailed in the last chapter.

The map to the treasure starts via the John 3:16 Path: "For God so loved the world that He gave his only Son, so that everyone who *believes* in Him might not perish but might have eternal life." Don't be afraid to take it because God doesn't expect you to be perfect. He does, however, expect you to at least *strive* for perfection. Your coach, Jesus, also reminds you of the finish line prize: "In My Father's house there are many dwelling places…And if I go and prepare a place for you, I will come back again and take you to Myself, so that where I am you also may be." [John 14:2-3] If the course gets too steep, Jesus also said in Matthew 11:28, "Come to me all you who are weary and burdened and I will give you rest." Finally, it's never too late to come to Christ: American philosopher, Dr. Mortimer Adler, became a Catholic at 97 years old.

How do I *train* to win Heaven?

Do these three things:

1. "Try to learn what is pleasing to the Lord [God]." [Ephesians 5:10] Without knowing what's pleasing to Him, you won't even know where the starting line is to compete for the prize of eternal life. (See God's good pleasures in the last chapter.)

2. Know your hurdles: those things that make you tired, tax your time, tempt you, and cause you to sin. *Gradually* remove or reduce hurdles from your path, such as:
   - Excessive time spent watching TV shows, movies or sports
   - Social media, fantasy sports or other internet overload
   - Alcohol or drug abuse
   - Sins against the commandments
   - Smut: in written, electronic, thought, word, or physical form
   - Preoccupation with house maintenance, pet care, work commute, yardwork, etc.
   - Sins of omission: not doing what you ought to do

3. Use 59 seconds at the end of each day to ask yourself: *How much time did I give to …*

    A) God?
    B) Others?
    C) Me?

Then, make progress monthly on waxing A and B.

Taking stock of your day is called *reflection* and, without it, your life is like a ship without steering or a captain without a compass. Socrates said this almost 2,500 years ago: "An unexamined life is not worth living." Reflection will keep you on track.

But if you still choose not to race, there's always the walk-in-the-woods with Wormwood and Screwtape.

What if I still don't feel God's existence?

For those still unsure if God exists, then the last chapter spoke only to your *mind*. You're a person who also needs to *feel* God's existence.

You're here because your brain knows there's overwhelming evidence for God, but your heart has not yet rested in Him. So, the hole in you still exists and can only be filled by an encounter with the Holy Spirit, who dwells within you. This heartfelt journey to Him must be sought, fought, and won because it takes a convinced heart to love God and neighbor. Each personal journey to God is unique. You arrive when *trust* in God is sealed and you drop your nets and commit to following Him. The head-to-heart trip has three common elements: a messenger, a message, and then a mission – vigorously practicing the Faith. If you conquer this trip, then your heart will be moved to action – to seek and find God. Be assured, He is waiting for you!

Here's what a journey looks like:

The messenger: my mom. At age 13, I had just 'graduated' from God through the Confirmation sacrament. My mom then surprised me with a meeting on the front stoop to inform me that I must continue religious studies by joining a youth group. I refused to join. She refused to yield – recalling her own mission to evangelize others. She then proposed that I simply *try* the group. I just wanted to end the battle-on-the-stoop. So, I agreed to go, but knew that I would win the war after attending just *one* youth group meeting.

The message: The youth group was in Smithtown, New York. It was populated with 13-year-old boys and girls, which provided enough common ground for me to stay for several meetings until *that* life moment.

Christmastime, 1973 – Lower East side, somewhere between the Bowery and the Hell's Angels home base [old photo below, near where we visited]

Our youth group leader, Mrs. Ragusa, took us on a journey into New York City to visit a facility that housed mentally ill youths. It was located in a building in the Bowery – skid row at the time – and near the home base of the Hell's Angel's motorcycle gang. Our leader also brought presents for these teenagers: a bar of soap wrapped in a washcloth. As a teenage boy, myself, this lame offering was a source of embarrassment to me. When we entered the facility, we were immediately greeted by many mentally-challenged youths and we presented each with a wrapped toiletry. I braced for their disdain and disgust towards our offering. But their reactions did not make any sense to me. They were *all* happy to get a present, unwrapped it with anticipation, and even smiled while holding the cloth and soap. My gift-giving embarrassment morphed into self-embarrassment. For these humble teenagers had collectively summarized the whole Christmas season by appreciating a simple gift of pure soap wrapped in cloth, just as the humble shepherds accepted the Holy One wrapped in swaddling clothes on that first Christmas day. I reflected on how much more I had than these teenagers – including my healthy, but immature brain – and firmly promised to start giving to others as a response to my own blessings. So, it took humble minds to humble me, and they – as well as Mrs. Ragusa's decision to take us into the bowels of poverty and human struggle – created a life-changing message for me that winter day in 1973.

The mission:

I began to fulfill my Bowery promise in my early twenties in the 1980s. I started by giving blood in my early working years in Piscataway, NJ. I also tutored a child in math and visited the sick at St. Peter's Hospital in New Brunswick, NJ.

I later became a Legion of Mary member, bringing prayers and goods to the poor. One visit was to a family whose father – a barber by trade – had passed away, leaving a mother with two daughters in their early twenties, one an epileptic. In the winter, they would literally live under blankets in a one-room flat with one 40-watt lamp for light. They had no heat because their money paid for the ill daughter's medication.

My volunteering continued at a New Brunswick, NJ, men's homeless shelter. This shelter was operated by the Brothers of Charity. I was humbled by the homeless men's conditions and their bunk-bed existence. This motivated me and others to create an annual variety show (based on the TV Gong Show) that ran for three years and raised $4,000 in total for the shelter's inhabitants. Later, I devoted a great deal of volunteer time to K-12 grade children, tutoring math, running chess clubs, coaching girls' softball and basketball, coaching boys' baseball and basketball, being a Cub Scout den leader and township recreation committee officer, and teaching Catholic Confirmation classes.

My energies were also spent in six months of training and 50+ miles of cycling in Sussex County, New Jersey, for the United Way; playing a euphonium for 15 Christmases with Salvation Army brass musicians at the red kettle; and playing in a community band for years, and at nursing homes at Christmastime. I'm also fortunate to be able to offer annual financial support for 30+ years for the Brothers of Charity, cover the schooling for five children in places like India, Guatemala, and North Africa – through Christian Foundation for Children and Aging (now Unbound.org); and continue my blood donations for 37 years and counting.

Still, my blessings significantly outweigh the little that I have accomplished. So, I continue to try to make myself useful toiling on this religious book as a first-time writer.

Fulfilling my life-long promise of charitable works has also given me sustained joy and validation over time. One year, on the last day of Confirmation class, after the students had left the classroom without even a simple goodbye (to my dismay), I was clearing my desk and was interrupted by a voice: "Mr. Young...". I looked up to find one student, Spencer Schaub, still there. He continued, "...thank you for teaching me about God." To that, I thought, "So shines a good deed in a weary world."

I have certainly come to *feel* God's presence in all of this. How? By the messenger (my mom) on the front stoop who wouldn't yield; by the teacher who took us to meet humble, mentally challenged youths who delivered a stunning message of appreciation; and by the years spent trying to do some good. These good works have given me peace and joy and the hope that I'm running towards a bright eternity.

Here's some advice from an older person:

A lukewarm Faith will kill you. True faith is felt by vigorously practicing it, using your time, talent, and treasure. If treasure is meager, then give time. Remember, too, as St. James reminds us, that "...faith without works is dead." (James 2:26). Also, these good works – these acts of love which must cost you something – must also be given to those *outside* of your inner circle: "For if you love those who love you, what reward do you have? Do not even the tax collectors do the same?" [Matthew 5:46]. And be patient and alert, for one day a messenger will cross your path – one that will ask you to do some good. You may be reluctant to grant their request. But if you pray about it and then acquiesce, both will lead you to perform random acts of kindness and acts of love, triggering a transformation of your heart. The latter phases – reluctance, kindness, love, and transformation – are seen in the compassionate (18-minute) short film, *Feeling Through*, where a homeless man encounters a deaf-blind man. This film exhibits the messenger-message-mission model. View it.

Finally, act to change your part of the world...instruct others along the way. No need to travel far, just bloom where you're planted...and humbly be a doer of the Word. And seek God, because He wants to be found, like the child in the following story:

A grandfather visited his grandson and asked him what he'd like to do. "Let's play hide-and-seek, grandpa." The grandfather agreed and said that he would count first. "...Eight, nine, ten...ready or not, here I come." But as the grandfather started looking, his grandson popped out and said, "Here I am!" The grandfather shook his head and explained that the game is not played that way, to which the grandson said, "But grandpa, *being found* is the most fun part of the game, so I just couldn't wait for you to find me..."

That's God's attitude towards you. He longs for you to seek and find Him. So, God often veils Himself in those with strong convictions, in humble people and neighbors in need. And when you run into God, you'll *feel* peace and joy – and love, which is His true presence. So, what are you waiting for? Fill the void in you with God.

Question #3: How do I get to Heaven?

Jesus Christ gave this answer: "Whoever believes and is baptized *will be* saved ..." (emphasis added) – Mark 16:16

He didn't say, "...is saved...", which would imply that salvation is attained in an instant in time. Rather, Paradise is granted through perseverance – a lifelong *pursuit* of trusting and obeying God, doing good deeds, being God's witness, and evangelizing others. Biblical evidence for faith-in-action as necessary for salvation is (paraphrased) here:

Matthew 25:31-46➔Jesus' *Judgment of the Nations*
Revelation 3:16➔...*if your faith is lukewarm, I [Jesus] will spit you out*
James 2:26➔   ...*faith without works is dead*

Mark 16:16 ➔the Map to Heaven. Here, in vine and branch form:

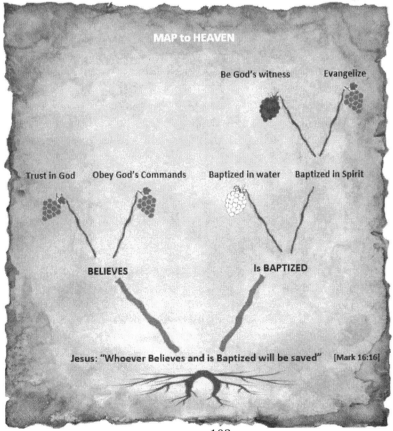

Heaven is yours if you flow through these branches and cultivate each with right living:

1. Trust in God, trust in His truths.
2. Obey God's commands.
3. Be baptized in water.
4. Be God's witness: imitate Christ's life through personal sacrifice in service to others. Seek only necessary comfort and be like a martyr.
5. Evangelize: bring others to God.

Here's a **GOOD** skeletal summary of the Map:

➜ Do what pleases God.

Fleshed out, here's a **BETTER** summary:

➜ Have a relationship with Jesus;
   obey God's commands;
   love your neighbor (charity).

Finally, the **BEST** short summary of the Map to Heaven, in acronym *PROC* – your process for getting to Heaven:

➜ PRAY–READ–OBEY–CHARITY

Remember: you follow the map, you get the treasure. And frequent travel along each branch (Baptism by water once only) is right practice for right living. Tip: just as amateur athletes study the pros, we should study the habits of the saints. Even better, imitate the "vine of life Himself": Jesus Christ.

Caution: Traveling the paths of the map may feel like a breathless trek to Mt. Everest's peak, as each path uncovers your old or maybe newly discovered sinful ways. But do not despair because all is possible for God, who says, "Do not fear: I am with you; do not be anxious: I am your God. I will strengthen you; I will help you..." [Isaiah 41:10] Also, help yourself: Get to know what pleases God ... work to remove your sinful hurdles ... and reflect on your progress.

Let's zoom in on each branch to lay bare your duties to God and neighbor. Go now to the starting blocks for an adventurous run…

Baptized in water:

Baptism is a Christian sacrament that removes original and personal sin – *all* sins.
It is an antibiotic for sin. Baptism is the
gateway to the Christian life of faith and
makes you a child of God – therefore an
heir – with the Holy Spirit dwelling within you.

Promises made at Baptism or Baptismal
renewals consist of renouncing Satan
and professing oneself as a child of the
Holy Trinity: God the Father, God the Son, and God the Holy Spirit.

Bishops, priests and deacons baptize, but in case of necessity, anyone – even a
non-baptized person – can baptize another using the Trinitarian (Holy Trinity)
baptismal formula and with required intentions.

Baptism is necessary for your salvation. But for those who die prior to it, Jesus'
Church acknowledges certain conditions under which a non-baptized person
can be saved.

Baptism purifies your soul and gives you sanctifying grace. You're now a clean
slate.

Baptism and Divine Mercy Sunday (described below), are displayed in the
end-of-book *Street Map to Heaven* illustration as **one of the 8 streets to Christ**.

BELIEVES: *"Whoever believes in the Son has eternal life, but whoever disobeys the Son will not see life, but the wrath of God remains upon him."* [Jn. 3:36]

This path *fork* – BELIEVES/belief in God – is fulfilled by a trust in God and in all of His teachings, and an obedience to His commands. So, prayer and obedience are the fruits of your belief in God. Let's visit each terminal branch.

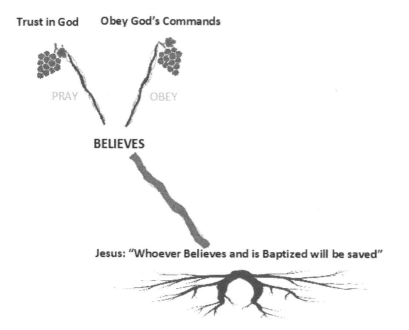

Trust in God   Obey God's Commands

PRAY   OBEY

BELIEVES

Jesus: "Whoever Believes and is Baptized will be saved"

Trust in God: *"Worry about nothing, pray about everything."*
[Philippians 4:6, paraphrased]

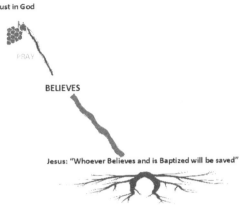

Your journey begins at this terminal (after an early Baptism) because belief and trust in God happen first, else why be a witness, evangelize, or obey?

Trust in God = Trust in His truths.

A short list of truths ➔ Our God is One in Three Persons: Father, the Creator of all things; Son, Jesus Christ, the Redeemer, who made Heaven accessible to us; and Holy Spirit, the One who dwells within us and makes us a holy temple. Evidence for the Father is seen in the physical universe; and in the likes of mathematics, music, and nature. Evidence for the Son, Jesus Christ, is seen in the biblical records and in His disciples' willingness to die proclaiming the risen Lord. And who resurrects himself but God? Finally, evidence for the Holy Spirit is at Jesus' Baptism in the Jordan, at Jesus' Transfiguration, and at Pentecost, where tongues of fire descended upon the apostles who then began to speak in foreign languages understood by the visiting, devout Jews from many regions. All could not believe their ears – a true miracle.

Trust in God consists of three things along this path:

I.   The first requirement to truly and fully trust in God is to believe that He exists as one God in three Persons. Chapter 1 gave overwhelming evidence for God.

II.   The second requirement to truly and fully trust in God is to believe that Jesus is God, believe that He rose from the dead, believe in *all* that His one, holy, catholic (universal), apostolic Church teaches, and believe that Jesus is truly in the consecrated Wine and consecrated Host: the Eucharist. These convince you to obey all His teachings and embrace His supreme offering of mercy:

Divine Mercy Sunday

Jesus visited a Sister Maria Faustina Kowalska, in Poland, starting on Sunday, February 22, 1931. She hand-wrote over 950 pages in six diary notebooks to document these visits. Jesus asked her to deliver a new message of hope to the world: *Divine Mercy Sunday*, a feast day – and the Octave of Easter – where participants would have all their sins and punishments removed. There is nothing more important for your soul than these two Sundays. Easter Sunday is where Jesus gave us the gift of eternal life – if we will accept it – and Divine Mercy Sunday prepares us for His second coming by making our souls spotless – like a second Baptism. And it's available annually to refresh the sinful soul! Let's be clear on the magnitude of this Feast through this dire example: a person who performs all Divine Mercy Sunday requirements and then dies suddenly will go directly to Heaven. Clarity is needed on three other points:

What are the requirements for all sins and punishments to be erased on Divine Mercy Sunday?

- ✟ You practice mercy in words, by forgiving or by comforting; in deeds; or in prayers toward others leading up to the feast. You also harbor no feelings of anger or bitterness.
- ✟ You trust that Jesus on that day will pardon you from all your sins and sin-related punishments → "Jesus, I trust in You."
- ✟ You go to Confession near the feast day.
- ✟ Free of mortal sin, you receive Holy Communion on that Sunday.

Why doesn't penance after a Confession remove all the punishments due to sins?

Because all of your lifetime Confessions and penances – taken together – were probably not perfect. What are the odds they were? Think of sins and their punishments like a wooden fence. Each sin puts a nail in your life fence. When you go to Confession, your sins are forgiven: the nails are pulled out, but the marks (punishments) remain. To remove these punishments, you must do penance. But over a lifetime, any imperfect penances/Confessions still leave marks on the fence. If you die with any sins or remaining punishments (but no mortal sins on your soul), you go to Purgatory, since nothing unclean can enter Heaven [Rev. 21:27], nor see the Lord [Hebrews 12:14]. Purgatory is where remaining sins and punishments are purged. Purgatory is not a family picnic – but after it, you do go to Heaven.

Aren't the benefits of this Feast equal to those granted in a plenary indulgence?

Yes, but plenary indulgences are harder to achieve, since you must be detached from sin, even minor sins. Is that even possible? Jesus gave us an easier path to total pardon, so **choose instead** Divine Mercy Sunday.

Divine Mercy Sunday's easy requirements set your soul at God's gate. Then it's up to you to stay camped at the gate by working to please Him through a process of **P**ray–**R**ead–**O**bey–**C**harity.

Notice what Jesus said about this Mercy Sunday:

- ✝ "Let the greatest sinners place their trust in My mercy. They have the right *before* others…"
- ✝ "Before I come as a just judge, I first open wide the door of My mercy. [But] He who refuses to pass through the door of [Divine Mercy Sunday] must pass through the door of My justice…"

III. The third requirement to truly and fully trust in God is that you develop a relationship with Him:

- ✝ You pray often. Better: you pray your way through the day. Dr. Robert A. Cook: "Pray before you answer the phone. Pray before you open a [text or email] …Pray before you sign a contract – God has already read the fine print. Pray before you go on a trip. Pray before you go on a date. Pray before you take a job or leave one. Pray before you decide to move or decide to stay. Pray before or during a situation. You'll find that God takes a hand in your life."
- ✝ You read the Bible. A Catholic Bible has 73 books and an imprimatur sign. Example: The New American Bible, Revised Edition (NABRE). The Bible is to be read as part of our pursuit to unwrap (accept) Jesus' offer to live with Him.

St. Isidore of Seville on the Bible: "When we pray, we talk to God; when we read, God talks to us." He also wrote, "The more you devote yourself to study of the sacred [scriptures], the richer will be your understanding of them, just as the more the soil is tilled, the richer the harvest."

Peter Kreeft on prayer: "I strongly suspect that if we saw all the difference even the tiniest of our prayers to God make, and all the people those little prayers were destined to affect, and all the consequences of those effects down through the centuries, we would be so paralyzed with awe at the power of prayer that we would be unable to get up off our knees for the rest of our lives."

A relationship with God means that you *go off-road* – from Satan's world of busyness, distractions, sin, and noise – to pursue prayer, reading, and silence. All three lead to reflection, and reflection is the gateway to God.

Jesus is your partner in prayer. He gives you the keys to the universe, and more, with these promises:

"…all things for which you pray and ask, believe that you have received them, and they will be granted you." [Mark 11:24]

"Ask, and it will be given to you; seek, and you will find; knock, and it will be opened to you." [Matthew 7:7]

Jesus guarantees answers to those who ask for good things. But remember, God doesn't answer prayers on a set schedule, so be patient, and be alert! For some prayers are answered in the wildest ways. For example, two people may be passing by you, talking out loud, and their conversation may contain the answer to your earlier prayer. Yes, it has happened.

Tips for praying:

✟ *Go to your room*. God prefers private prayer. Or treat your car as a sanctuary for prayer. But Jesus also said: "…where two or three are gathered together in my name, there am I in the midst of them." [Matthew 18:20] That's why public Mass is where *Heaven meets Earth*.

✟ *No robots*. Think of the words in prayer, else it is not sincere, but just vain repetition and babble. Sincere prayer is heard by God, else the prayer is dead. Caution: prayers like the Our Father and Hail Mary may become robotic. Say these prayers again as if for the first time!

✟ *Pray for God's Name, Kingdom, and Will be done:*
Begin with God's interests before yours; glorify His Name; and do His will on Earth. Whatever you're doing right now or later, do *everything* for the glory of God. [1 Cor. 10:31].

✝ *Pray with a forgiving spirit towards others:*
Shed anger towards others and humbly empty yourself before praying.

✝ *Don't be wimpy:* Be bold and persistent in prayer. (Think of Abraham talking God down from punishing Sodom – that's bold.) Also, hand over to God your most difficult problems, then sleep like a baby.

How and what to pray – wrapped in an acronym:

Perfect prayer to God consists of prayers of adoration and praise; thanksgiving; petition; intercession; and silence or simply waiting on God. Petition is a prayer for yourself; intercession, one for others. You must first empty/humble yourself before prayer – a useful phrase is: "Lord, have mercy on me, a sinner." To which God may reply, "At your service", or "AtYoService" or "ATYOS".

ATYOS ➔ a prayer acronym (and **one of the 8 streets to Christ**):
Adoration, Thanksgiving, Yourself, Others, and Silence.

Daily Prayer Process – using ATYOS and sample prayers:

1) Go to a very quiet place.
2) Prepare to be with God: inhale-exhale slowly 12 times.
3) Make the sign of the cross and say: "Lord, have mercy on me…a sinner."

Now pray words like:

[A] "God, you're all-powerful, all-merciful, all-loving; the one true GOD"
[T] "Thank you for the blessings for me, my family, and…"
[Y] "Lord, help me to be patient" and "God, what's your plan for my life?"
[O] "God, help [name(s)] to seek and find you, for the sake of their soul."
[S] …be silent …listen …wait on God to speak to you.

Finally, *reflect:* How much time did I give to God? To others?

PRAYERS ON THE ROAD TO ETERNITY

The Lord's Prayer [Our Father] ➔ Jesus debuted it in the Sermon on the Mount – with seven petitions to the Father:

Our Father, Who art in Heaven, hallowed be Thy Name
➔ May Your Name be kept holy, not used in vain, and known by all.

2nd Petition: *Thy Kingdom come*
➔ May Jesus come again and take us to Heaven.

3rd Petition: *Thy will be done on earth as it is in Heaven*
➔ May we follow the Golden Rule and do God's will like angels and saints.

4th Petition: *Give us this day our daily bread*
➔ May God give us today what we need for our body and soul.

5th Petition: *...and forgive us our trespasses, as we forgive those who trespass against us*
➔ May God forgive us the same way that we forgive others.

6th Petition: *...and lead us not into temptation,*
➔ May God help us to resist sin and temptation.

7th Petition: *...but deliver us from evil. Amen.*
➔ May God deliver us from the evil one: Satan. So be it!

The Lord's Prayer: see it again for the first time ➔ Know well each petition. Why? Because Jesus gave us this prayer, and it pleases God when we say it.

Sign of the Cross – *In the name of the Father, and of the Son and of the Holy Spirit, Amen.*

So simple and powerful: Acknowledges the Trinity's presence in what you're about to pray. It's a mark of discipleship (I deny myself, I pick up my cross, and follow you, Jesus); it's a defense against the devil; and it even helps reduce feelings of anger, lust, and fear. Singular *name* because three Persons in *one* God.

The Apostles Creed – it came before the fully-assembled Bible and summarizes our belief in the Trinity:

I believe in God, the Father Almighty,
Creator of Heaven and earth, and in
Jesus Christ, His only Son, our Lord,   ➜ Jesus is God
who was conceived by the Holy Spirit,
born of the Virgin Mary,   ➜ Jesus is also human
suffered under Pontius Pilate,
was crucified, died and was buried;
He descended into hell;
on the third day He rose again from the dead;
He ascended into Heaven, and is seated at
the right hand of God the Father Almighty;
from there He will come to judge the living and the dead.
I believe in the Holy Spirit, the Holy Catholic Church, the communion of saints, the forgiveness of sins, the resurrection of the body, and life everlasting. Amen.

Decade Prayer to Jesus – The Virgin Mary gave the three Fatima shepherds this to pray at the end of each Rosary Decade:

"Oh My Jesus, forgive us our sins, save us from the fires of Hell, lead all souls to Heaven, especially those in most need of Thy mercy."

Come Holy Spirit: a prayer so old it can't be traced. Here, abridged: "Come, Holy Spirit, fill the hearts of your faithful and enkindle in them the fire of your love…"

"Come, Holy Spirit!" ➜ A short directive to the Spirit when you need inspiration or courage.

Why pray to the Holy Spirit? Because He created and lives in you and gives you courage and wisdom, if you would only ask Him. Theologian and mystic, Meister Eckhart, on the Spirit [Breath] of God within: "If you are convinced that who you are at the deepest level is one with God then all of the trials and tribulations of life will not bother you; they cannot touch you at the deepest level." Now that's worry-free living. Here are other Holy Spirit résumé credentials that should convince you to enlist Him to work *within* you:

✞ Created the Roman Catholic Church in AD 33 at Pentecost, 50 days after Jesus rose.

✞ Is the 3rd Person of the Triune God, so is infallible.

✞ Spoke to and instructed humanity through about 73 prophets over thousands of years.

✞ Said 2,600 years ago [Jer. 1:5] that a soul is imparted on a baby at conception: "Before I formed you in the womb I knew you, before you were born I dedicated you…"

✞ Inspired the Catholic Church to include 46 Old Testament books and 27 New Testament books into the Bible: 73 total books. The Protestant Bible has seven less books and was created in the 1500s. Question: could the Holy Spirit have been *wrong* on the Bible's contents for over 1,000 years before being corrected by a human named Martin Luther?

Glory Be: an ancient prayer reminding us of the Mystery of the Trinitarian God. The rosary form is:

Glory be to the Father and to the Son and to the Holy Spirit, as it was in the beginning, is now and ever shall be, world without end. Amen.

➔ *World without end:* God's Kingdom in Heaven never ends.

Hail Mary: a prayer that reveals a love story between humanity and the Father, mother, and Son of God. Just prior to the Angel Gabriel's visit to Mary, humanity is sinning more than loving God and neighbor. The Designer of the universe has given mankind free will; an imperfect human nature; and lets Satan roam the Earth – three strikes against the world, but God knows He can combat the three by sending down the One: Jesus Christ. God's message, however, of love and humility cannot be delivered by a hypocrite – a warrior God – so Jesus is born as a baby in a stable with smelly animals and sweaty shepherds as honored guests. And who is going to believe Jesus' Gospel unless He Himself experiences the full burden of humanity – temptations, struggles, torture, and death? Else, anyone could say, "I've gone through as much" or "I've seen worse." So, Jesus is born in squalor, soon after escapes death and flees with family as refugees to the Egyptian desert, returns to Nazareth to live as a poor carpenter's son, later fasts for 40 days in a desert, then walks the earth as slave labor – no vacation days – serving and teaching others. At His performance review, He is rewarded by being tortured, ridiculed, crucified, given vinegar to drink and then stabbed after death. He responds to it all with meekness; like a lamb, an example of true humility and love. A perfect Triune Person to deliver the Good News of the Gospel: The Kingdom of God is here and I'll die to pay your entrance fee.

But God's Son-of-Man Incarnation plan hinges on a sinless, teenage girl saying yes to it. The *Hail Mary* prayer is a thanks to Mary for her yes. For without it, there's no believable God-man Jesus. The prayer also thanks Jesus as a Savior Who willingly dies and rises to pay for our sins and to give us a chance at Paradise. The prayer also asks Mary to intercede for us sinners.

Marian truths. Catholics don't worship Mary as a god. But we do pray to her to help lead us to her Son, Jesus, and we ask her to ask Jesus to grant our prayer. Why don't we simply pray directly to Him? We do, but there are times – like at our death! – where Mary as our proxy pleading our eternal life case to Jesus may be a lifesaver for us. And He listens to her. Proof? Read the *Wedding at Cana* [John 2].

The Hail Mary: see it again as if for the first time.

Hail Mary, full of grace, the Lord is with thee;
➜ From the Annunciation: Angel Gabriel greets Mary.
Verse meaning: Father, thank you for your salvation plan (sinless Mary carrying Jesus in her womb).

Blessed art thou amongst women, and blessed is the fruit of thy womb, Jesus.
➜ From the Visitation: Elizabeth greets Mary.
Verse meaning: Mother Mary, thanks for your yes, and thank you Jesus, for being my Savior.

Holy Mary, Mother of God, pray for us sinners, now and at the hour of our death. Amen.
➜ Verse meaning: Mary, intercede and ask Jesus to save us. So be it!

For Heaven's sake – yours – commit to memory the *meaning* of each verse.

Pause: before visiting the mother of all prayers below, let's talk truth. Prayer is said to the Triune God, Virgin Mary, holy angels and saints – all in the living, invisible world. Some discount prayer or think it might be a waste of time. You, too? Then answer this: what brainless part of the invisible world is fully trusted and always working for you? But failure of it causes death in seconds? It's *GRAVITY*. We so depend on it that no one ever wakes to ask if it's going to be a good gravity day or not. It's a continuous force that grounds us and even keeps the planet whole. No gravity, no planet, no us. If this *brainless, invisible* force is so useful, then how infinitely more trusted and responsive to us must be the *living, invisible* world. After all, could a non-living thing out-serve the God of the universe? Let's believe your sincere prayers are received by heavenly Hosts with joy. Earthlings: boldly pray with confidence. It *is* heard and so stirs into action the living, invisible world – all at your service.

The Rosary – the mother of all prayers is a summary of the Gospel and Christ's life. It is 20 Mysteries where Jesus walks through all of the Map-to-Heaven paths before expecting the same from us. The rosary's takeaway is in its last sentence: "That meditating on these Mysteries [of Jesus' life] we may imitate what they contain and obtain what they promise [Heaven]…" **Translation**: Imitate Christ and you will be given eternal life. Also imitate the Mysteries by:

✟ Becoming holy and shining your light like in Jesus' own Transfiguration.

✟ Practicing Sorrowful Mysteries like carrying your cross, experiencing agony and suffering through worldly work, and accepting ridicule for being Christ's follower.

✟ Trying to bring God's Kingdom to wherever you go.

✟ Starting your earthly ministry as Jesus did in the Temple.

✟ Obeying the Holy Spirit Who came down and has taken residence in you.

The rosary is also a spiritual sword made by God and is effective in the battle against evil. As we arise daily to constant, worldly distractions, Br. Daniel María Klimek reminds us of life's true wakeup call:

"Life's a battle between two kingdoms: between the Kingdom of Heaven and the kingdom of hell, between God and the devil… And, what's most urgent not to neglect, is the reality that we're *all* born into this war and thus called to be soldiers on the battlefield."

Servant of God, Dolindo Ruotolo (1882-1970), was such a soldier, sleeping less than three hours a night because of his devotion to God. He describes the rosary in irresistible terms:

"The decades of the rosary…are like the belt of a machine gun: every bead is a shot [at Satan]." Every said bead also ejects a speck of sin from your soul, like a shooter marble does to a *duck* in a marbles game. Further, every said rosary decade is a progression against Sin and Satan (the SS), the true terror group hounding you. Both evils must be crushed underfoot.

Some select benefits for praying the rosary:

✠ Mary: The soul which recommends itself to me by recitation of the Rosary shall not perish.

✠ Mary: I'll deliver from purgatory those who've been devoted to the Rosary.

✠ A rosary decade said with family is *glue* because the family that prays together stays together.

Below are rosary instructions (enhanced from newadvent.org). Memorize rosary prayers and Mysteries in order to regularly say the rosary while driving solo in your (sanctuary) car or taking solo walks – this cultivates a relationship with God and the Virgin Mary. Finally, guard against robotic chants of each decade's 10 Hail Marys by thinking of the verse meanings as you go: Thank-you to a) the Father for His salvation plan, b) the mother's yes, and c) the Son's yes in being our Savior.

How to pray the Rosary

1. SAY THESE PRAYERS...

IN THE NAME of the Father, and of the Son, and of the Holy Spirit. Amen. *(As you say this, with your right hand touch your forehead when you say* Father, *touch your breastbone when you say* Son, *touch your left shoulder when you say* Holy, *and touch your right shoulder when you say* Spirit.*)*

I BELIEVE IN GOD, the Father almighty, Creator of Heaven and earth. And in Jesus Christ, His only Son, our Lord, Who was conceived by the Holy Spirit, born of the Virgin Mary, suffered under Pontius Pilate; was crucified, died, and was buried. He descended into Hell. The third day He rose again from the dead. He ascended into Heaven, and sits at the right hand of God, the Father almighty. He shall come again to judge the living and the dead. I believe in the Holy Spirit, the holy Catholic Church, the communion of saints, the forgiveness of sins, the resurrection of the body, and life everlasting. Amen.

OUR FATHER, Who art in Heaven, hallowed be Thy Name. Thy kingdom come, Thy will be done on earth as it is in Heaven. Give us this day our daily bread, and forgive us our trespasses, as we forgive those who trespass against us. And lead us not into temptation, but deliver us from evil. Amen.

HAIL MARY, full of grace, the Lord is with thee. Blessed art thou among women, and blessed is the fruit of thy womb, Jesus. Holy Mary, Mother of God, pray for us sinners, now and at the hour of our death. Amen.

GLORY BE to the Father, and to the Son, and to the Holy Spirit. As it was in the beginning is now, and ever shall be, world without end. Amen.

O MY JESUS, forgive us our sins, save us from the fires of Hell; lead all souls to Heaven, especially those in most need of Thy mercy. Amen.

ANNOUNCE each mystery by saying something like, "The third Joyful Mystery is the Birth of Our Lord." This is required only when saying the Rosary in a group.

HAIL HOLY QUEEN, mother of Mercy; our life, our sweetness, and our hope. To thee do we cry, poor banished children of Eve. To thee do we send up our sighs, mourning and weeping in this vale of tears. Turn, then, most gracious advocate, thine eyes of mercy toward us. And after this, our exile, show unto us the blessed fruit of thy womb, Jesus. O clement, O loving, O sweet Virgin Mary. Pray for us, O holy Mother of God, that we may be made worthy of the promises of Christ. Amen.

O GOD, WHOSE only-begotten Son by His life, death and resurrection, has purchased for us the rewards of eternal life; grant, we beseech Thee, that by meditating upon these mysteries of the Most Holy Rosary of the Blessed Virgin Mary, we may imitate what they contain and obtain what they promise, through the same Christ our Lord. Amen.

2. IN THIS ORDER...

INTRODUCTION
1. IN THE NAME...
2. I BELIEVE IN GOD...
3. OUR FATHER...
4. HAIL MARY...
5. HAIL MARY...
6. HAIL MARY...
7. GLORY BE...
8. O MY JESUS...

THE FIRST DECADE
9. ANNOUNCE...
10. OUR FATHER...
11. HAIL MARY...
12. HAIL MARY...
13. HAIL MARY...
14. HAIL MARY...
15. HAIL MARY...
16. HAIL MARY...
17. HAIL MARY...
18. HAIL MARY...
19. HAIL MARY...
20. HAIL MARY...
21. GLORY BE...
22. O MY JESUS...

THE SECOND DECADE
23. ANNOUNCE...
24. OUR FATHER...
25. HAIL MARY...
26. HAIL MARY...
27. HAIL MARY...
28. HAIL MARY...
29. HAIL MARY...
30. HAIL MARY...
31. HAIL MARY...
32. HAIL MARY...
33. HAIL MARY...
34. HAIL MARY...
35. GLORY BE...
36. O MY JESUS...

THE THIRD DECADE
37. ANNOUNCE...
38. OUR FATHER...
39. HAIL MARY...
40. HAIL MARY...
41. HAIL MARY...
42. HAIL MARY...
43. HAIL MARY...
44. HAIL MARY...
45. HAIL MARY...
46. HAIL MARY...
47. HAIL MARY...
48. HAIL MARY...
49. GLORY BE...
50. O MY JESUS...

THE FOURTH DECADE
51. ANNOUNCE...
52. OUR FATHER...
53. HAIL MARY...
54. HAIL MARY...
55. HAIL MARY...
56. HAIL MARY...
57. HAIL MARY...
58. HAIL MARY...
59. HAIL MARY...
60. HAIL MARY...
61. HAIL MARY...
62. HAIL MARY...
63. GLORY BE...
64. O MY JESUS...

THE FIFTH DECADE
65. ANNOUNCE...
66. OUR FATHER...
67. HAIL MARY...
68. HAIL MARY...
69. HAIL MARY...
70. HAIL MARY...
71. HAIL MARY...
72. HAIL MARY...
73. HAIL MARY...
74. HAIL MARY...
75. HAIL MARY...
76. HAIL MARY...
77. GLORY BE...
78. O MY JESUS...

CONCLUSION
79. HAIL HOLY QUEEN...
80. O GOD, WHOSE...
81. IN THE NAME...

3. WHILE TOUCHING THESE BEADS TO
   KEEP TRACK OF YOUR PROGRESS...

G.B. J. A. O.F.
^Repeated^

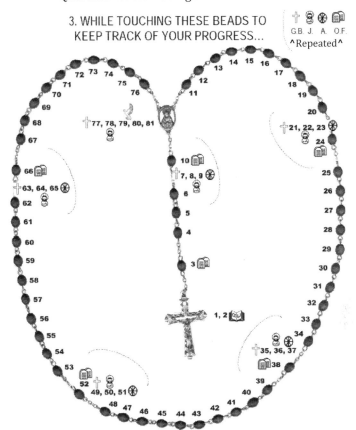

4. AND SILENTLY MEDITATING ON THESE "MYSTERIES",
   OR EVENTS FROM THE LIVES OF JESUS AND MARY...

On Monday and Saturday, meditate on the "Joyful Mysteries"
First Decade (Steps 9-22): The Annunciation of Gabriel to Mary (Luke 1:26-38)
Second Decade (Steps 23-36): The Visitation of Mary to Elizabeth (Luke 1:39-56)
Third Decade (Steps 37-50): The Birth of Our Lord (Luke 2:1-21)
Fourth Decade (Steps 51-64): The Presentation of Our Lord (Luke 2:22-38)
Fifth Decade (Steps 65-78): The Finding of Our Lord in the Temple (Luke 2:41-52)

On Thursday, meditate on the "Luminous Mysteries"
First Decade: The Baptism of Our Lord in the River Jordan (Matthew 3:13-16)
Second Decade: The Wedding at Cana, when Christ manifested Himself (Jn. 2:1-11)
Third Decade: The Proclamation of the Kingdom of God (Mark 1:14-15)
Fourth Decade: The Transfiguration of Our Lord (Matthew 17:1-8)
Fifth Decade: The Institution of the Holy Eucharist (Matthew 26)

On Tuesday and Friday, meditate on the "Sorrowful Mysteries"
First Decade: The Agony of Our Lord in the Garden (Matthew 26:36-56)
Second Decade: Our Lord is Scourged at the Pillar (Matthew 27:26)
Third Decade: Our Lord is Crowned with Thorns (Matthew 27:27-31)
Fourth Decade: Our Lord Carries the Cross to Calvary (Matthew 27:32)
Fifth Decade: The Crucifixion of Our Lord (Matthew 27:33-56)

On Wednesday and Sunday, meditate on the "Glorious Mysteries"
First Decade: The Glorious Resurrection of Our Lord (John 20:1-29)
Second Decade: The Ascension of Our Lord (Luke 24:36-53)
Third Decade: The Descent of the Holy Spirit at Pentecost (Acts 2:1-41)
Fourth Decade: The Assumption of Mary into Heaven
Fifth Decade: The Coronation of Mary as Queen of Heaven and Earth

Obey God's Commands:

"If you love Me, you will keep My commandments." – Jesus [John 14:15]

"If you wish to enter into life, keep the commandments." – Jesus [Matthew 19:17]

Here, we'll cover the Holy Trinity command sets:

- God the Father's 10 Commandments.
- God the Son's new commandment: *Love one another. As I have loved you, so you also should love one another.* [John 13:34]
- God the Holy Spirit's five [inspired] Church Precepts.

I. God the Father's 10 Commandments (10 Cs):

Relevant for 3,500 years and counting, here are the 10 Commandments' summary statements:

➔ You shall love the Lord your God with   [Sums the first 3]
   all your heart, soul, mind, and strength.
➔ You shall love your neighbor as yourself.   [Sums the last 7]

The 10 Cs' math equation is: LAW = LOVE

But how do commandments – the Law – show God's love for us? To know, think like Him:

You love your people, so you want them to be happy. Billions of people interact in millions of collective ways, so you create commandments that, if followed, will lead to no conflict. As obedience to the rules increases, the world's collective happiness increases. Here's one law of love that supports the latter premise: *Thou shalt not commit adultery.*

Follow all 10 Cs and you will be truly free from sin, not a slave to it. But obeying all *10* may not be simple because to claim self-mastery and victory over them, the God of the universe must acknowledge that you have virtually satisfied this requirement:

"...be perfect, just as your heavenly Father is perfect." – Jesus [Sermon on the Mount, Matthew 5:48]

You may wonder, "How can I obey all 10?" You can't alone, but can with God – so pray throughout the day for help.

Further, you ask, "Where do I begin?" First, you must get to know *all* facets of each Commandment, else you will land on the road to ruin. Second, for those stubborn sins of idols, addictions, and the flesh, try *fasting* – self-denial develops self-control. Finally, ask yourself this one question when making moral choices:

In what I'm thinking/saying/doing *right now*: **What would Jesus do?**

The quest-for-perfection challenge also requires that you memorize the rules. This acronym may help you:

10 Commandments ➔ 10 Cs ➔ 10 Chicks ➔
10-letters in '*GLASS CHICK*'

GLASS CHICK is **one of the 8 streets to Christ**.

10 Commandments

The 10 Cs are mainly life's *DO NOTs*, so the GLASS CHICK acronym will start with 'No-':

No-**G**ood, **L**ying, **A**dults **S**teal the **S**abbath...

Coveting & **H**onoring **I**dols' **C**ursed **K**illings

G: Good ➜   You shall not covet your neighbor's goods
L: Lying ➜   You shall not bear false witness against your neighbor
A: Adults➜   You shall not commit adultery
S: Steal ➜   You shall not steal
S: Sabbath➜   Remember to keep holy the Sabbath day – the Lord's Day

C: Coveting ➜ You shall not covet your neighbor's wife
H: Honoring➜ Honor your father and your mother
I: Idols ➜   I am the Lord your God, you shall not have strange gods before Me
C: Cursed ➜   You shall not take the name of the Lord your God in vain
K: Killings ➜   You shall not kill

Memorize the 10 Commandments using the *GLASS CHICK* phrase, and you'll have another tool in your prepare-for-Eternity tool belt. Use the phrase to also assess sins prior to going to Confession.

But there's more: The Commandments' fine-print will surprise, instruct, and humble you. Post the next pages in a place you frequent. Then do a thrice-reading of them. That will aid your quest for becoming a better Christian. And call on Jesus to help you because He said, "…without me you can do nothing.", and, "If you remain in me and my words remain in you, ask for whatever you want and it will be done for you." [John 15:5,7]

10 Commandments:

1. I am the Lord your God, you shall not have strange gods before Me ➔
   Strange gods: **anything/anybody** that addicts or consumes you, or acts like an idol to you, or consumes too much of your time at the expense of God or neighbor. Examples may be:
   - Money, materialism, alcohol, drugs, sex, viewing pornography, gambling
   - Social media consumption, texting, emails, celebrity followings, being a groupie
   - TV, video games, fantasy sports, watching sports

   Other things that go *against* the first commandment:

   - Witchcraft/wizardry/fortunetelling/superstitions/mediums/spells/omens/ horoscopes
   - Mistreating sacred persons/places/things [all a sacrilege]
   - Worshiping saints/Mary/statues. It *is* OK to pray to them to intercede/pray for us *to* God
   - Presuming you can save yourself without God, or believing God won't help save your soul
   - Taking part in non-Catholic *worship* or [some] marriage types; or rejecting/insulting the Catholic faith as laid down by Jesus and His Church. Remember: Jesus, the Church, and the Magisterium's teachings are all perfect, but all people who administer the Faith are fallible. This point will help prevent you from abandoning your Faith solely over faulty administrators.

2. You shall not take the name of the Lord your God in vain ➔
   - Never use the precious name of Jesus or God's name in frustration, anger or exclamation (including the words "god d_mn"); this is sinful and insulting to God (blasphemy).
   - It's a sin to curse or use profane words
   - It's a sin to make rash, unjust, and unnecessary oaths, and to lie under oath (perjury)

3. Remember to keep holy the Sabbath day – the Lord's Day ➔
   - Always go to Mass on Sundays and Holy Days of Obligation when humanly possible
   - Avoid violent/vulgar/vixen-filled music/books/video games/movies/events on this day
   - Avoid shopping and buying things on Sunday – careful planning can help you accomplish this
   - Do spend time with family/friends or helping others with their issues/problems
   - Avoid unnecessary business work and physical labor

4. Honor your father and your mother ➜
- Respect them always; and obey them while you're living under their roof
- Respect them even if they have lost their mind to dementia/Alzheimer's diseases
- Respect others in *lawful* authority, too, e.g., bishops/priests/teachers/bosses/police/others

5. You shall not kill ➜
This commandment forbids the killing only of human beings. Abortion is an example of killing. Killing when defending oneself against an attacker doesn't break this commandment. You must also **avoid** these:
- Killing in your heart: Fighting, anger, hatred and revenge
- Being a bad example or causing scandal, both of which can induce others to sin
- Killing your body: Suicide; also using, or using in excess, things like cigarettes/alcohol/drugs
- Killing potential: Reckless or intoxicated driving or other bad habits that could kill you/others
- Killing the *rightful* freedoms of others

6. You shall not commit adultery ➜
- Jesus said looking lustfully at another is committing adultery in your heart
- Only consensual sex with your spouse is allowed
- No masturbation, no oral sex, no pornography, no prostitution, no raping
- You must maintain pure thoughts, words, actions, and looks towards others
- It is a sin to listen to immodest conversation, songs or jokes when you can avoid them
- You must dress modestly
- You must avoid viewing bad-faith and immodest: books, social media, websites, newspapers, magazines, films

7. You shall not steal ➜   These are all forms of stealing:
- Stealing *anything* that doesn't belong to you
- Cheating on taxes, tests, school homework, etc.; also, taking credit for another's work
- Illegally downloading music
- Depriving someone of their rights or goods; knowingly receiving or sharing stolen goods
- Giving or taking bribes
- Doing bad work, supplying bad materials, or wasting time while working for others
- Destroying others' property; also, failure to report destruction/stealing is also stealing
- Receiving money or goods under false pretenses

- Borrowing stuff and not making an effort to return it
- Not sharing resources (food, shelter, and clothing) with others who need it
- Deliberately wasting planet resources, for example, wasting water or electricity

8. You shall not bear false witness against your neighbor ➜

   Against this commandment are:

   - Lying and swearing to a lie. Note: If you don't lie, you don't have to have a good memory!
   - Gossiping about another can't be 100% true/verifiable, so avoid doing it
   - Being a hypocrite: promising one thing, but then doing something else
   - False praise and boasting are similar to lies
   - You must speak the truth in all things, and must be careful of the honor/reputation of others
   - Rash judgments [believing a person is guilty of sin without just cause]; backbiting [saying evil things about another in their absence]; slanders [telling lies about someone with the intention of hurting them]. To stop this sin in you, recall this: *Let he who is without sin cast the first stone.*
   - Telling persons what others have said unkindly about them; this can lead to bad consequences
   - Everyone has a right to a good reputation, so give people the benefit of the doubt and speak up in their defense. After all, it's almost impossible to restore a damaged reputation.

9. You shall not covet your neighbor's wife ➜

   - Do not desire, entertain bad thoughts, nor look lustfully at your neighbor's spouse. [This commandment is on impure *thoughts*]

10. You shall not covet your neighbor's goods ➜

    - Do not *envy* your neighbor's good fortune or their better position in life
    - You are forbidden to desire to take or keep wrongfully what belongs to another
    - This commandment deals with envious and dishonest *thoughts* against a neighbor

Every six months, try this exercise: Pick one commandment to work on and improve your thoughts/words/deeds on it.

In five years, you will have made a valiant effort toward passing all 10 Cs. What next? Try the exercise again.

Finally, be encouraged by this: Half the Commandments – 2, 3, 4, 9, and 10 – can be conquered by simply creating *good habits*. Read Lao Tzu's previous words on habits (found in Topic #19).

II. God the Son's new Commandment ➜ *Love one another. As I have loved you, so you also should love one another.* [John 13:34]

"Always remember to love your neighbor; always prefer the one who tries your patience, who tests your virtue, because with her you can always merit…"   – Blessed Mary of Jesus Crucified

"I really only love God as much as I love the person I love the least." – Dorothy Day

Jesus wasn't speaking of feelings, but a *commitment* to others. *Others* mean neighbors and strangers, too. Here's the math for Jesus' new command:

LOVE = CHARITY ➜ freely giving to the poor, ill, or helpless.
     "Give to everyone who asks of you." – Jesus [Luke 6:30]

LOVE = ACTS of **humility** (e.g., washing feet; doing dirty jobs), **sacrifice**, **suffering**, **pain**, or even **death** for the benefit of others.

LOVE = Being a servant to others ➜ Live-to-Give ➜
     Giving your life as a gift to others.

LOVE = Willing good to another simply for their own sake.

The supernatural, root equation for all above is: LOVE = GOD

LOVE is **one of the 8 streets to Christ.**

We share in the very life of God when we love and our acts put us in touch with Him. Further, true greatness lies in the humble commitment and service to others:

"The *greatest* among you must be your servant." – Jesus [Matthew 23:11]

Note: do not mistake an act of *kindness* for an act of *love*. A quick story reveals the difference: One morning, with two $20 bills in hand, you travel into town to visit its Main Street shops and later have lunch. You find a person traveling on foot pushing a bicycle that holds all of his belongings.

Act of kindness: You decide to give him one $20 bill, and the other you use to buy your own lunch.

Act of love: You give him both $20 bills and you are hungry until dinner.

Furthermore, acts of love trigger in you humility, sacrifice, suffering, pain, or even death for the good of another. Acts of love *cost you* something – in time, talent, or in treasure that's part of your *need*. Note: giving $$ from your *want* doesn't really cost you anything, so it's not an act of love – but this giving is still good.

How do we practically live out this new commandment? Ease into it first: Start with simple acts like saying 'hello' to someone and being of good cheer, helping out in the kitchen, assisting a sibling with their homework, helping an elderly neighbor with their chores, or volunteering time at your parish. Then, build momentum over time to slowly move from self-centeredness to selflessness. Later, move to total and complete detachment from self – mastery over Commandment #1 is key here: NO IDOLS! Finally, your apex goal may be like that of Saint Teresa of Calcutta: 'Love until it hurts.'

But wait. Let's just start by understanding the core of the new Love commandment ➜ Mercy.

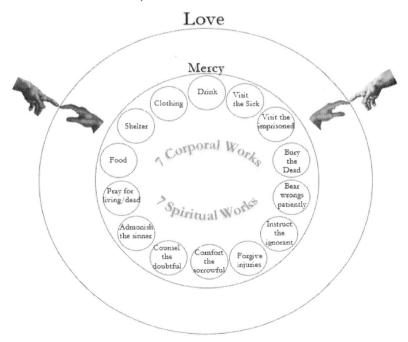

The 14 Works of Mercy (One of the 8 streets to Christ)

Mercy is: taking pity on an unfortunate person, or, pardoning an offender (by not giving them justice). Jesus spoke of the end times in His Judgment of the Nations discourse [Matt. 25], where the Son of Man comes and separates people into 2 flocks: the sheep, and the goats. Only the sheep will inherit the Kingdom of God because they performed works of mercy toward others, while the goats will not. Jesus mentioned a handful of the mercies, and the Catholic Church defined the rest of the 14 based on Jesus' teachings, parables and commands.

Here is what's important to you: Jesus will judge us on how much we have loved God and others through our merciful acts. So, we must prepare to do these acts by strengthening ourselves in mind, body, spirit, discipline, and in the talents that God has given us. For you, that means this: strive to become a multi-tooled player for Christ. Become the best version of yourself. But you may ask: where in Paradise does it say that I must hone my skills? Jesus packs the answer in the two-pronged parable He gave just prior to His sheep-and-goats discourse – in the Parable of the Talents [Matt. 25:14-30, paraphrased]:

"A master planned a journey, so he called in his servants to entrust his goods to them. He gave five talents [money] to one; two talents to another; one talent to a third – each according to his ability. Then he went away. The first servant invested the five and made five more. The second servant invested two and made another two. But the third man went off and buried his one talent. The master finally returned. Upon seeing that the first two servants had increased his monies, he said, 'Well done, good and faithful servants. Since you were faithful in these matters, I'll give you greater responsibilities. Come, share your master's joy.' The man who buried the one talent said, 'Master, I knew you were a hard person, so out of fear I buried your talent. Here it is back.' His master said, 'You wicked, lazy servant! You should have put my money in the bank to make interest on it. Now then! Take the talent from him and give it to the one with 10. For to everyone who has, more will be given and he'll grow rich; but from the one who has not, even what he has will be taken away. And throw this useless servant into the darkness outside, where there's wailing and grinding of teeth.'"

This parable starts with a master who **a)** imparts gifts "to each according to his ability" and ends with **b)** 'For to everyone who has, more will be given and he'll grow rich; but from the one who has not, even what he has will be taken away.' What do these mean?

a) God gives us human talents that He wants us to *invest* (grow) and *use* over time to build up His Kingdom on Earth.

b) The Kingdom is built up by doing acts of mercy toward others; and "...to everyone who has [given mercy to others], more [of God's mercy] will be given [to them] and they'll grow rich; but from the one who has not [given mercy], even what they have [of God's mercy] will be taken away [and they'll receive justice instead]." Proof that our acts of mercy increase God's mercy on us is also found in the Beatitude: "Blessed are the merciful, for they shall receive mercy." – Sermon on the Mount [Matthew 5]

Here are some suggestions for effective works of mercy:

- [Life-long] Educate yourself in a vast number of worldly skills for later use and benefit to others.
- Study the Christian faith to prepare to evangelize, instruct, and inspire others to seek God.
- Become adept at generating wealth for later use to serve and support the poor.
- Use internet sites to learn how to repair things to later aid your neighbors.
- Exercise/build strength over time to extend your physical capabilities to help others in emergencies.
- Plan your *live-to-give* lifestyle for the sake of others. For example:
  o Buy and have a house generator ready-to-go to help neighbors during power outages.
  o Put spare $$ and non-perishable food in the car glove box or carry $$ or gift cards to give to the needy.
  o Store 50/50 antifreeze in your vehicle to hand out to people with over-heated vehicles.
  o Learn to knit/sew; and in your spare time, produce clothing for others.
  o Learn a second language to instruct even more people about God and His Kingdom.

Finally, here are the two Mercy sets, acronyms for each (both quirky-but-memorable), and practical, worldly examples of how to satisfy each mercy – 14 more tools for your prepare-for-Eternity tool belt.

7 Corporal Works of Mercy: How to remember them: an army corporal is asked to babysit a whiny, fidgety child. The **corporal** is babysitting a fussy (**FSS**) kid (**CIDD**).

Corporal Mercies acronym ➜ *FSS CIDD*

F: Give **F**ood to the hungry.
S: Give **S**helter to the homeless.
S: Visit the **S**ick

C: Give **C**lothing to those in need.
I: Visit the **I**mprisoned.
D: Give **D**rink to the thirsty.
D: Bury the **D**ead.

Recall alternative: Start by remembering the well-known phrase, 'food, shelter, clothing, drink', then only three mercies remain. Two require you to visit people: the sick and imprisoned. That leaves the dead: bury them.

Practical ways to think about and act on each corporal (physical body) mercy:

The basic corporal mercies consist of local acts:

- Always have $$ on hand to donate to a cause or person in need.
- Work at a shelter or food pantry.
- Collect and deliver clothing to the poor.
- Visit, email, call, or mentor adults/teens in a hospital or prison.
- Run a drink stand and give away the proceeds.
- Pay for, go to, or provide support (meals, house maintenance, prayers for the deceased) for a funeral for an acquaintance or poor family.

Think and act globally, too. Consider this: The needy exist everywhere, especially when natural disasters occur. But the truly needy exist in countries where people live on $2 a day. It is there where your donated resources affect the most people. For example, the Unbound organization educates children who live outside the USA for about $40 a month. Contrast that with the USA's education cost per child: $1,000 per month. So, one can support more easily an overseas child's education, which helps break the cycle of poverty in their family.

Think and pray about it, while considering this wise saying, again from St. Teresa of Calcutta:

"Poverty is not made by God, it is created by you and me when we don't share what we have."

Listed below are unusual, extreme, or off-the-beaten-path ways to think and act on most corporal mercies. This large list is given to fully support your pursuit of goodness and contains guaranteed opportunities to help others and yourself when you later meet Jesus Who will say (paraphrased): "Well done, good and faithful servant! ... whatever you did for one of these least brothers of mine, you did for me."

Corporal Works of Mercy (examples)

Food	✟ Play word games at freerice.com to donate rice to the world's people.
	✟ Daily cook/deliver homeless meals, like Narayanan Krishnan: an award-winning chef at a 5-star hotel who saw on the street a man eating his own human waste. Mr. Krishnan decided "this is what I should do the rest of my lifetime." He's now cooked 1.5 million meals in 12 years for India's destitute. He said: "Now I'm feeling so comfortable and so happy. I have a passion, I enjoy my work…this is the purpose of my life.": https://www.cnn.com/2010/LIVING/04/01/cnnheroes.krishnan.hunger/index.html
	✟ Do social media food drives; give food gift cards to the poor & ask to pray for them.
	✟ Use charitynavigator.org to donate $$ to a highly-efficient food bank – maybe one whose CEO isn't compensated.
Shelter	✟ Donate or volunteer at Catholic Charities or Habitat for Humanity.
	✟ Buy a generator, then lend it to neighbors without electricity; or invite them over.
	✟ Volunteer at local homeless shelters.
	✟ Help those in your neighborhood by using Nextdoor.com.
	✟ Use charitynavigator.org to donate $$ to a highly-efficient shelter – maybe one whose CEO is not compensated.
Clothing	✟ Knit or sew hats/scarves/blankets; like the late 91-year-old man who'd knitted 8000 hats: https://www.facebook.com/humankindvideos/videos/1271174672918179/
	✟ Join social media orgs to knit or crochet in your spare time for the homeless: https://www.craftsy.com/knitting/article/crocheting-and-knitting-for-charity/
	✟ Buy fewer clothes and donate the money difference to the poor.
	✟ Make knitted hats for the homeless, each in 30 minutes with this machine: https://www.youtube.com/watch?v=iIXHN1KNGOU/
Drink	✟ Use your vacation time to travel and build a well for a community.
	✟ Conserve water and other resources as a good citizen of the world.
	✟ Buy lifestraw.com/doing-good web products to give safe water to the world; also buy and send Grayl Ultralight Water Purifier bottles to Africa/Asia.
Sick: visit them	✟ Be a multi-annual and lifetime blood donor to aid those who have blood disorders.
	✟ Volunteer at a nursing home or hospice, giving the people your carefree timelessness.
	✟ Bring a sick person soup or food.
	✟ Take care of *any* needs related to the medically sick who are at home or in the hospital.
Imprisoned: visit them	*People can be imprisoned in mind, body, or circumstance.*
	✟ **In mind:** Dementia/mental issues/loneliness imprison people in mind. Volunteer to help these people, visit them, be a suicide hotline helper, or take care of other needs.
	✟ **In body:** physical disabilities or old-age imprison some and restrict their mobility or capabilities. Spend time with them and give them appropriate help.
	✟ **In circumstance: a)** being forced to work multiple jobs, **b)** stranded on a roadway, **c)** being forced into slavery or held captive, **d)** kids can't go to school: family too poor to afford it, are all examples of imprisonment. Help for each: **a)** babysit for or mentor the adult to help them get one good job; **b)** call 911 or provide roadside help [in a safe way]; **c)** volunteer at crisis or child protection centers, **d)** donate $$ to educate overseas kids.
	✟ Prevent circumstantial imprisonment. E.g., take Virtus® training to help prevent child abuse; go to 4help.org (411 service of hotlines) to choose/join a help hotline; carry (in car) pre-mixed antifreeze and a jump starter to aid stranded motorists; carry food gift cards to give out to the homeless; be proactive: report *any* environmental safety hazards

7 Spiritual Works of Mercy: How to remember them: The Holy Spirit doesn't lie; the Spirit doesn't fib; the **Spirit** doesn't *pack* (**PACC**) *fibs* (**FIB**). **Spiritual** Mercies acronym ➔ *PACC FIB*

P: **P**ray for the living and the dead.
A: **A**dmonish (spiritually caution) the sinner.
C: **C**ounsel the doubtful.
C: **C**omfort the sorrowful.

F: **F**orgive injuries done to you.
I: **I**nstruct the ignorant.
B: **B**ear wrongs patiently.

Spiritual Works of Mercy (practical ways to satisfy each)	
Pray for the living and the dead	✞ Use ATYOS prayer model, outlined above, to say prayers for 'O' others.
	✞ Pray a rosary for a family member or friend in need.
	✞ Pray Jesus' Divine Mercy Chaplet for the souls in Purgatory.
	✞ Have a Mass said for someone deceased.
Admonish the sinner [Mt. 18:15]	✞ First, get *yourself* in order: Remove the wooden beam from your own eye; & speak with this in mind: 'Let he who is without sin cast the first stone'– Jn.8:7
	✞ Balance admonishment with diplomacy and encouragement.
	✞ Just do it: God expects us to correct others, and it'll get easier over time.
	✞ Keep love in mind & talk about your own failures before correcting others.
	✞ Stand up for what you believe in.
	✞ Be respectful and explain kindly why you disagree with others' behavior.
Counsel the doubtful [Mt. 28:19]	✞ First get to know your Catholic faith well.
	✞ After building trust, ask others: "How's your relationship with God?"
	✞ Pray to the Holy Spirit to guide you to give wise advice.
	✞ Reassure others: God is always with you, loves you, & answers your prayers.
	✞ Be positive and encourage others to put their hope and trust in God.
Comfort the sorrowful	✞ Ask, 'How are you?', then listen carefully; follow-up if your gut tells you to.
	✞ *Listen* to another share their hardships.
	✞ Reach out and do a favor(s) for those whom you know are suffering.
Forgive injuries [Mt. 6:14]	✞ Release any grudge or resentment.
	✞ Pray for the person who offended you: pray the Divine Mercy Chaplet.
	✞ Tough forgiving? Think: 'God, forgive them because they don't have a clue'.
	✞ Remember: a person has seriously wronged you, and if you don't let go and forgive, they're harming you a second time [while they sleep like a baby]. So, forgiveness is more for you: peace for you, & God rewards peacemakers.
Instruct the ignorant [Mt. 28:19]	✞ Learn the Catholic Faith, then teach religious education or Bible study.
	✞ Instruct others by *example*: simply go about living a holy life.
	✞ Explain the faith to your friends.
Bear wrongs patiently [8th Commandment; Mt. 6:14]	✞ Don't start on the defensive; assume there's a reason for a person's action.
	✞ Pray for the person irritating you.
	✞ Overlook others' mistakes, try not to be critical, assume the best in others.

Peacemaking and Service: All 14 acts of mercy are acts of peace felt by the one receiving mercy or indirectly experienced by those surrounding them. Likewise, a peacemaker is a person who performs a service, so all peacemaking acts are services. And all acts of mercy and peacemaking (both declared Beatitudes), and service toward others, are acts of love. The diagram below includes all of these. It also includes your devoted *time, talent,* and *treasure* to acts of Mercy, acts of Peacemaking (Ti-P, Ta-P, Tr-P), acts of Service (Ti-S, Ta-S, Tr-S), and direct acts of Love (Ti-L, Ta-L, Tr-L). We'll discuss the three T's next.

Time, Talent, Treasure (TTT)➔ 3 Dimensions (3D) of Love:

Time is the most precious present to give to others. Time can also be used to develop your talent, that which makes your acts of love more effective. Further, time *and* talent generate treasure – goods and money – to be given away for others' sake. So, every act of love is produced by one or a combination of these three items. It should be your lifelong goal to free up a good deal of time, develop many talents, and become adept at creating wealth, all to help build up God's Kingdom. Work on this 3D goal every month. Alert: acts of love must also be your duty to neighbors or strangers, and *especially* to those who can't repay you.

Here are example acts of TTT related to **peacemaking**:

Ti-P: Time you give fostering peace to help to resolve a conflict among family members.
Ta-P: Negotiating talent applied to reaching an agreement between, for instance, two townships.
Tr-P: Giving $$ to facilitate a peace pact between two groups.

Example acts of TTT related to providing **service** to others:

Ti-S: Time given to repair an item, like a leaky pipe, for a neighbor.
Ta-S: Mentoring/training an adult or child of a poor family in skills such as math, finances, or construction.
Tr-S: Donating a building that will be used to provide a place for free medical services for the poor.

Here are example acts of TTT related to **love**:

Ti-L: Time spent with a young boy or girl through Big Brothers or Big Sisters programs.
Ta-L: Using your organizing/musical/financial talents to create a benefit show where proceeds go to the needy.
Tr-L: Donating your car to a poor family.

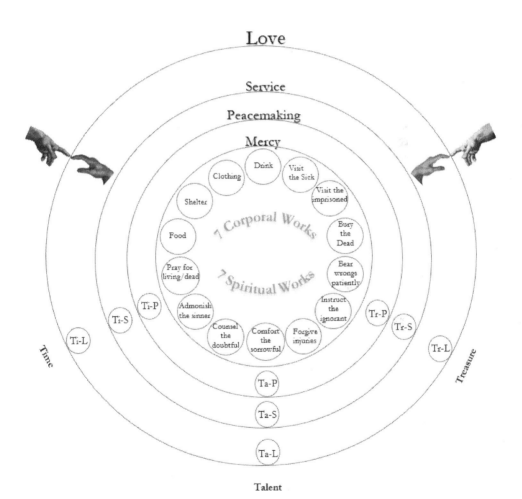

The Ripple Effects of Self-centeredness versus Love:

Ripples of self-centeredness: John was harsh with his wife one morning, and this upset her. Her daughter, Maria, sensed her mother's sadness while being driven to school. Maria was dropped off and then promptly ran into her new friend, Beth, who had just transferred to the school. Maria – bothered by her mom's mood – preceded to treat Beth poorly. Beth later went home and told her own mom that she was treated badly at school by a new friend. Her mom promptly said to her husband, "See, we shouldn't have put Beth into this unwelcoming school, so let's begin the process of moving her out of there."

Ripples of love [a true story]: Dylan Siegel was in first grade when he learned that his friend, Jonah, had a rare liver disease with no known cure. Dylan decided to write a book to help raise money to find a cure. In one week, his book profited $5,000. But he wanted $1 million, so with the help of his parents, they used media outlets to tell the story of one boy trying to help his friend to survive. In two years, the $1 million goal was met. Doctors then planned to use the money on human gene therapies, saying, "We are on the verge of curing or treating this disease, and that would not have been possible if a six-year-old boy hadn't created this book."

Love is like Light ➜ a particle and a wave: A good act starts a ripple – a wave – through a chain of people. A student of mine once reported this effect when his father paid the car toll for the person behind him, which caused a chain of like payments until their own car lost sight of the toll booth. This proves that we are built for love, and we don't know how many people will be affected by the wave we initiate. So, choose your words and actions wisely – choose acts of kindness, choose to love. Moreover, the gospel of John says that God is both *light* and *love*. We also know that *light* is a particle and a wave. Is *love* the same? Yes, God designed it just like light: an *act* of love is like a particle that spreads like a wave. And when the wave hits a target (person), it's like any physical wave: some bounce (appreciation) off the target back to the source, some (love) is absorbed by the target, and some (love) passes through the target to others. Think about it.

LOVE ONE ANOTHER [Agape Love]: *A pool analogy*

Picture a crowded swimming pool with five diving boards at various heights. You're on a 20th-floor balcony, so the largest board is the highest above the pool. Each diver chooses a board, executes a dive, and lands in one of four circles. The swimmers below are refreshed in degree by a diver's splash from a given height. The splash radiates outward as a wave until it hits the edge of the pool.

This analogy describes well the effect on others of **Agape Love**. Its *effort types* are defined by the diving boards named: Humility, Pain, Sacrifice, Suffering, and Martyrdom. Larger boards equate to potentially greater acts of executed love. The four pool circles are Agape Love's *classes*: Mercy, Peacemaking, Service, Love. Your effort [act] of love lands somewhere in the pool. If your act lands in Mercy, for example, its resultant wave provides mercy to some, then radiates outward giving peace, too, as a service and as love itself. Finally, your act of love always touches God.

~~~~~~Agape Pool~~~~~~

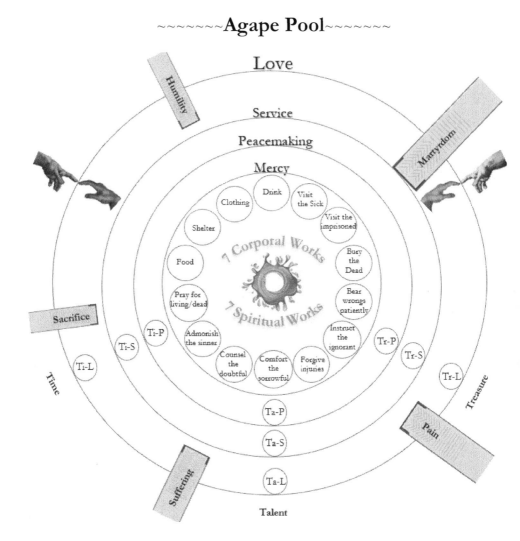

The above map also contains these insights:

✝ Acts of martyrdom are rare but when they occur, their love is vast and their story is told for generations. Proof? Jesus' dying and rising for us created the Catholic Church and followers numbering in the billions. And during the Vietnam War, in separate incidents, 60 soldiers each fell on a grenade to save their fellow soldiers. It's quite possible that these soldiers were able to make the supreme sacrifice because their lives were built upon many heroic moments of self-giving.

✟ God highly values mercy and expects us to show mercy towards others. Proof? Jesus spoke of mercy in: The Our Father (Matthew 6:9-13) [forgive us our trespasses as we forgive those who trespass against us], a Beatitude (Matthew 5:7) ["blessed are the merciful for they shall receive mercy"], Parable of the Talents (Matthew 25:14-30) [to everyone who has given mercy to others, more of God's mercy will be given to them], Parable of the Good Samaritan (Luke 10:29-37) [describes specifically how we should show mercy], Parable of the Rich Man and Lazarus (Luke 16:19-31) [the *eternal* cost of not showing mercy], and Divine Mercy Sunday [a gift of mercy as a full pardon to those who participate in this special day]. Mercy is also a form of peacemaking, a service to others, and an act of love. So, you hit the bullseye and create the biggest wave of Christian love when you perform one of the 14 acts of mercy!

✟ We *must* forgive others for their perceived or actual wrongs against us, else we give God the permission to not forgive us in the same way. This deal is in the Our Father prayer. So, we risk everything if we don't forgive others. Likewise, we *must not* judge others (i.e., pass a final, non-changing judgment on them), else we permit God to judge us. So, we risk everything if we continue to judge others. Proof that both are true? Jesus said, in Luke 6:37: "Stop judging and you will not be judged. Stop condemning and you will not be condemned. Forgive and you will be forgiven."

Finally, a wise man once said: "Be kind. [For] everyone you meet is carrying a heavy burden." This saying is good, but not great. It speaks more of words than actions. We can improve on it to better align with Jesus' new commandment:

"Everyone you meet is carrying a heavy burden. So be loving and lighten their load."

III. Obey God's Commands: The 5 Precepts of the Catholic Church.

Before listing the precepts, let's ask some questions: Why must we listen to the Catholic Church? And, must we obey *all* its teachings, like those on abortion, contraception, and euthanasia; or, instead, be permitted to choose only those that we wish to obey? Answers are in the details:

✟ Jesus Christ created the Catholic Church: "…you are Peter, and upon this rock I will build my church, and the gates of the netherworld shall not prevail against it…" [Matthew 16:18]

✝ Jesus gave the church power over us, saying to Peter, the first Pope: "Whatever you bind on earth shall be bound in Heaven. And whatever you loose on earth shall be loosed in Heaven." [Matthew 16:19]

✝ God the Holy Spirit guides the Church, which was born on Pentecost, 50 days after Jesus' Resurrection. Pentecost began the apostles' mission to spread the Good News: Jesus is God, and by His dying on the cross and His rising from the dead, He has given us a chance at eternal life.

✝ There are many occasions in the saints' lives where Jesus gave them a directive, but then a Church superior forbade it. Each time, Jesus wanted the superior's orders obeyed over His own! St. Margaret Mary Alocoque experienced this: when she obeyed her religious superior over Jesus, He said, "I love obedience, and without it no one can please Me."

Conclusion ➔ Obey the Church = Obey God. Caution: when you feel the urge to ignore a Church rule, ask yourself: is my knowledge on this topic superior to 2,000 years of Catholic scholars' teachings? Shouldn't you at least probe until you understand *why* the Church teaches what she does?

The 5 Precepts of Jesus Christ's Catholic Church – necessary requirements for being a Catholic:

✝ You shall help to provide for the needs of the Church.   **(F)**

✝ You shall confess your sins [via the sacrament of Reconciliation] at least once a year.   **(R)**

✝ You shall observe the days of fasting and abstinence established by the Church.   **(A)**

✝ You shall attend Mass on Sundays and on Holy Days of Obligation (or attend any valid Vigil Masses) and rest from servile labor.   **(M)**

The 6 Holy Days are:

- January 1, the solemnity of Mary, Mother of God.
- 6th Thursday after Easter Sunday, the solemnity of the Ascension.
- Aug. 15, solemnity of the Assumption of the Blessed Virgin Mary.
- November 1, the solemnity of All Saints.
- December 8, the solemnity of the Immaculate Conception [Mary's own conception in her mother's womb].
- December 25, solemnity of the Nativity of Our Lord Jesus Christ.

✝ You shall receive the sacrament of the Eucharist at least during the Easter season.   **(E)**

The *5 Precepts* acronym, *FRAME*, is **one of 8 streets to Christ**.

We must surely obey Christ's Church, but what are the reasons why we *must* go to Mass, receive Communion, and go to Confession? Look below:

Why must I attend Mass every Sunday [and Holy Days]?

Mass is called the Lord's Supper because we feast on Jesus' Word in Bible readings and on Jesus Himself in the Eucharist. The Mass rubric has been the same since AD 155, and we're required to attend Mass per all Persons of the Trinity. One statement is from God the Father, four from God the Son, and one inspired by God the Holy Spirit:

1. You shall attend Mass on Sundays… [Church precept, inspired by God the Holy Spirit]
2. "Do this in memory of me." – Jesus [Luke 22:19]
3. "…unless you eat the flesh of the Son of Man and drink His blood, you do not have life within you. Whoever eats My flesh and drinks My blood has eternal life…" – Jesus [John 6:53-54]
4. The Parable of the Great Banquet – Jesus [Luke 14:15-24]
5. The Parable of the Wedding Feast – Jesus [Matt. 22:1-14]
6. "Remember the Sabbath day – keep it holy." – God the Father's 3rd Commandment [Ex. 20:8]

Still want to pass on Mass? Then talk to the legless woman in Africa who is known to have crawled 2.5 miles to get to Sunday Mass. For she knows that Jesus is truly there: "Where two or three are gathered in My name, there am I in their midst." [Matthew 18:20] Further, His presence is really in the consecrated Host and wine, so the priest at Communion is not a human Pez dispenser of bread wafers, but a giver of *God* Himself to make us a living tabernacle. How can we not see it that way? And how can we leave Mass and not do something astounding for others that day or week? Shouldn't it compel us to leave Mass and not just go shopping, out to eat, or home to tend the garden, but to go out and be the *change* the world needs? Dorothy Day of the Catholic Worker buried a coffee cup that had been used to hold the consecrated Hosts during a Mass. She knew what the Host truly *is* and its effect on anything (anybody) that it touched. Proof of what's really eaten by us is in a monstrance, *right now*, in Lanciano, Italy, where Jesus' AB blood type is all over its heart flesh and blood globules.

His death on the cross is re-presented at every Mass, for you. He is dying for *your* sins, to give *you* a chance at a great eternity. But you have to be present each week to *witness* His death for it to count as mercy. Else you get His justice at the moment of death.

Bishop Fulton Sheen said: "If you don't get anything out of Mass, it's because you don't bring the right expectations to it – like spiritual hunger. The Mass is not entertainment. It's worship of the God Who made us and saves us. It's an opportunity to praise God and thank Him for all that He has done for us."

Mass is a channel that opens between Earth and Heaven. We are surrounded by angels and saints each time the Blessed Sacrament (consecrated Host) is held up by the priest. Jesus is truly at Mass, and He's waiting to meet you, one-on-one.

What are the consequences for our children if we stop going to Mass?
James Stenson says: "Our ancestors risked persecution, even death, to be able to take part in Mass. When you have children someday, they'll need the graces and strength that come from the Mass. If you fail to pass it on because of your own indifference, you'll do the gravest injustice to them and to God. You have the power to snuff out, in one generation, the faith that has sustained your family for generations. This is an enormous responsibility. You will …answer to God for it."

Good arguments above for Mass attendance, but they're not enough. You also need to understand Mass elements and where they came from to make Mass more meaningful for you.

Appreciate and focus on each Mass as if it's your last: Think of Jesus at the church door greeting you and reminding you to meet Him at the end of *this* Mass for your life's final judgment. How will that upcoming appointment with Jesus affect the quality of your worship?

Sad news first: Mass attendance isn't your ticket out of hell. If you just go to Mass but don't use its fruits each week, you're lukewarm, and you know what Jesus said about that: Rev. 3:16. *Lukewarm* is like being a quarterback who goes into a huddle, breaks, then runs to the sideline without running a play. Instead, take Sunday treasures from Mass and use them to travel the week's charity map paths: *Evangelize* and *Be God's Witness*.

Joyful news: Mass is where we truly meet Christ. Jesus instructs us with His Gospel, then nourishes us with His true body and blood. Mass is where Heaven meets Earth, so we must dress appropriately: no T-shirts, shorts, overly casual outfits or ones imprinted with bad ideas. Wouldn't you, after all, dress well to meet the Queen of England? Then how much better for the King of the Universe?

Boldly say the Profession of Faith as if you were among Christ's early followers: It was risky business being an early Christian after Christ's Resurrection. Twenty-eight out of the first 31 popes up until AD 312 went to their deaths. Saying the Profession of Faith to the Holy Trinity could get you in trouble with Roman leaders. Christian persecutions were sporadic, but when they did occur it meant that Christians were used as human torches [by Nero in AD 60s] or fed to wild animals in the Coliseum or killed if they refused to denounce Christianity by sprinkling incense to Roman gods.

Today, Christians, like those in Egypt or in the Middle East, are threatened with similar persecutions. You can show solidarity with these people by boldly professing this faith message!

The word *Mass* means this: *to send or dismiss*, so truly go out after Mass and do your mission because God has a plan for each person's life. But if you don't do your plan, then it doesn't get done. Note: unexecuted plans are everywhere today. Proof? Just look closely at the world; it is such a mess. A *Catholic Mass Map* follows. It lists Mass parts and what to think/say/do in each. Commit these to memory and pass them on to children/family members to experience every Mass like it's your *last* one.

Catholic Mass Map:

Boring priest, bad music, crying babies. No matter. To get one step closer to Heaven, I come for God's Word and the Eucharist. MASS: its significant events, in order...	And what I, a churchgoer, thinks/says/does during each...
Once a week I pause everything, get ready, travel to church, and participate in Mass.	To love is to give 2 hours in 112 waking hours/week for God. Jesus gave His life to give us the Mass. He commands us: "Do this in memory of Me." Attendance at Mass avoids mortal sin, removes venial sins and lets God know His business is more important than mine.
When entering church, I solemnly dip fingers in Holy Water and make the Sign of the Cross.	As I dip, I say, "I reject Satan." I make the Sign of the Cross, then say, "I belong to God." Holy Water reminds me of my Baptism and its promises.
I study the Readings summary paragraph or the actual Readings prior to Mass.	My understanding of the 3 upcoming Readings is increased and they become more interesting/useful to me.
The priest enters Mass down the main aisle and heads towards the altar.	I liken this to Jesus' Palm Sunday entrance into Jerusalem for His impending Last Supper, Passion and Death – for my salvation. The priest stands in the person of Christ during the Mass.
Penitential Act: "I confess to almighty God, and to you my brothers and sisters, that I have greatly sinned ..."	I confess that I'm a sinner and ask all in the universe: Mary/angels/saints/the living, to pray for me and for me and my eternal happiness.
I say the Kyrie: " Lord have mercy... Christ have mercy..."	(Said in Greek by the early Christians) I ask God to save my soul "God, have mercy on me, a sinner."
Music throughout the Mass...	Its harmonies remind me of how I should live in harmony with others.
I say or sing the *Gloria*. "Glory to God in the highest, and on earth peace to people of good will ..."	A hymn first sung by the angels at Christ's birth in Bethlehem. How can I not give glory to the all-powerful/knowing/loving/merciful God who gives me everything?
LITURGY of the WORD begins: I listen to the 1st reading	This reading is usually from the Old Testament, which foretells New Testament things.
Responsorial Psalm: I say (or sing) it out loud	The psalm is the oldest part of the Mass and dates back before Christ.
LITURGY of the WORD continues: 2nd reading	This reading ties in with the first and is usually from the time *after* Christ ascended into heaven, e.g., from the Acts of the Apostles, or from the Letters of St. Paul.
I sing the Gospel Acclamation: "Alleluia...alleluia...alleluia"	Alleluia means "Praise God!" and this acclamation announces the Gospel (Word of God) is about to be read.
LITURGY of the WORD: GOSPEL reading	Jesus instructs and gives me the road map to Heaven ↑ I hope for Heaven and the room He's preparing for me.

The HOMILY: the priest further explains today's Readings	I listen intently, for the priest's Homily explains God's Word, which transforms me.
PROFESSION OF FAITH: I join in and say it out loud	Nicene/Apostles Creeds (in AD 250s, people raised death to believe in them). I pray them boldly; it's what I believe!
Prayer of the Faithful: We offer prayers, then say "Lord, hear our prayer."	We pray for the world and Church. Jesus is present and answers us because He said, "Ask and you shall receive", and "...where 2 or 3 gather...there am I with them."
LITURGY of the EUCHARIST: Eucharistic Prayer Preface	"...Lift up your hearts. We lift them up to the Lord..." I enter into Heaven at this moment (according to Revelation 4:1-2)
Eucharistic Prayer Preface (the Hymn of Victory) ↑ "Holy, holy, holy, Lord..."	"Holy, holy, holy, Lord God of Hosts. Heaven and earth are full of your glory..." ↑ I repeat this while in heaven with the angels and saints.
Eucharistic (Thanksgiving) Prayer	We're all at the foot of the cross as we re-present Christ's Crucifixion – we have a death sentence for our sins, but He has decided to die in our place. We have to be present weekly for Him to remove our death sentence.
"Take this all of you and eat of it, for this is My Body..."	The first RINGING of the BELLS ↑ My God is now on the altar, truly present in the consecrated Host.
The Great AMEN (at the end of the Eucharistic Prayer)	Amen here means, "I believe what I just heard and would stake my life on its truth."
The Our Father (The Lord's Prayer, which Jesus gave us in His Sermon on the Mount)	I say this because Jesus commanded me to. I ask for 7 things in it – it is a summary of the whole Gospel.
Sign of Peace	With this, I demonstrate my desire to make peace with my neighbor prior to receiving Jesus in Communion.
"Lamb of God you take away the sins of the world, have mercy..."	I say this because Jesus is the new Lamb of God being offered for sins and salvation.
"Lord I am not worthy that you should enter under my roof, but only say the Word and my soul shall be healed."	This is the Roman Centurion's great faith message that Jesus marveled over: "Lord I am not worthy that you should enter under my roof, but only say the Word and my servant shall be healed." I say our version with the same vigor.
COMMUNION: I receive the true Body and Blood of Christ; it's not a symbol, it is truly Him! So, I'm transformed and can never be the same again.	I must eat His flesh and drink His blood in Communion (Jn. 6), but cannot have It if mortal sin is on my soul! I receive the King in a home-made throne, then I say while eating the Host: "Live like Jesus." After kneeling, I sit and talk to Jesus for a while.
CONCLUDING RITE: The dismissal from Mass	Mass only ends when we are dismissed. Mass means "to send or dismiss"; so, I'm now being sent out to do my mission on earth, living like Christ, dying through suffering/sacrifice/pain, rising as a saint: "...go forth, to love and serve the Lord."

Why must I go to Confession [participate in the sacrament of Reconciliation]?

"Come, and go to Confession and make your peace with God." – St. John Bosco [paraphrased]

Confession is a requirement of Jesus' Catholic Church. Moreover, the Sacrament of Reconciliation was instituted by Jesus on Easter Sunday night. This sacrament gave the apostles and their lawful, apostolic successors the authority to administer confessions – in the Person of God – and give pardon for any confessed sins. Jesus created this sacrament by saying this to the apostles:

"As the Father has sent Me, so I send you…[while breathing on them] Receive the Holy Spirit. Whose sins you forgive are forgiven them, and whose sins you retain are retained." [John 20:21-23]

Mortal sins require that you receive this sacrament, and these sins must be absolved before you may receive Holy Communion. Confession also removes venial sins – those are *also* forgiven by prayer, fasting, works of mercy, and Holy Communion.

The sacrament of Reconciliation forces you to think about your serious sins, and your sinful omissions (the *good* you neglected to do as parents, family members, citizens, public servants or other potential role models) and state them all to the priest to reconcile and remove sin from you. This formal process is needed because nothing unholy will see the Lord. [Hebrews 12:14] The latter Bible passage, as well as many others listed at the following website location: https://www.ncregister.com/blog/darmstrong/25-descriptive-and-clear-bible-passages-about-purgatory, are evidence for Purgatory, where any remaining sins will be removed from us upon death. Unworthy Confessions over your lifetime will not lead to complete holiness. Either worthy lifetime confessions, prior-to-death participation in Divine Mercy Sunday or Purgatory after death will produce the holiness required to see God.

Finally, before receiving the sacrament of Reconciliation, use the 10 Commandments and the 5 Precepts of the Church to assess your sins, and the 14 Works of Mercy to assess sins of omission. These steps will prepare you for better confessions.

You shall observe the days of fasting and abstinence established by the Church:

✝ You *must* fast on Ash Wednesday and Good Friday.

✝ You *must* abstain from eating meat on Ash Wednesday and Lenten [pre-Easter] Fridays; and also, every Friday of the year *only* if meat abstinence is your preferred way to perform required, Friday penance. For a very thorough explanation on Friday penances, go to: https://CanonLawMadeEasy.com/2009/03/05/are-catholics-supposed-to-abstain-from-meat-every-friday/

✝ You must observe Sunday's Holy Communion rule: Don't eat or drink one hour prior to Communion.

Best wishes on your walk with God on this ***BELIEVE…Obey God's Commands*** path. Yes, it has many detailed steps. Just concentrate on making slow and steady progress. Don't give up if you sometimes fail. Realize that this path is doable with the right guide: Jesus Christ. Remember: this is about loving a God who loves you as if you're the only person in the entire universe.

Baptized in Spirit:

"Amen, amen, I say to you, no one can enter the kingdom of God without being born of water and Spirit." – Jesus [Jn. 3:5]

"God has created me to do Him some definite service. He has committed some work to me which He has not committed to another...He has not created me for naught...I shall do His work." – St. J. H. Newman

Above, Jesus calls Peter to walk with Him. Likewise, God by our side calls us into a missionary life: "...before you were born, I dedicated you." [Jer. 1:5] Peter acts while those in the boat look on. This image aptly depicts the Parable of the Sower's human roles of tourists and pilgrim. Peter's image also is an icon for Baptized in Spirit – the path *fork* (above right) which demarks our pentecostal *moment*, when the Holy Spirit enflames us with His seven gifts (e.g., wisdom and fortitude). These embolden us to kick down the door of *Fate* and go out into the world to fulfill our unique, preordained plan. Further, Baptized in Spirit's two paths – *Be God's Witness* and *Evangelize* – comprise our (sacrament of Confirmation) mission of *social justice*, in which we interact with sinners and aid oppressed peoples. Some other Socialite had this mission on Earth; now it's ours. Don't want it? Then you'll later arrive poorly dressed at the Divine Wedding Feast. But if you accept it, you'll live a life in Christ to the fullest, with adventure and some shouts of, "Wow, what a ride!" Ready? Kick down the door.

What is social justice? It's the view that everyone deserves fair treatment and equal opportunities. It's also the Golden Rule in action, increasing happiness in others as it promotes these:

- Life (by speaking out against abortion, euthanasia, and the death penalty)
- Marriage and family (by protecting the core unit)
- Human rights (by pursuing for all fair wages, safe spaces, and healthcare; and by working to end war, human and drug trafficking, slavery, and prostitution)
- 700 million poor who live on $1-2 a day (by improving their lot through education, better jobs, and microlending)
- Solidarity (by increasing justice and peace via political actions and fellowship)
- Earth (by acting and encouraging others to protect/preserve natural things)

Social justice: progress in it gives *hope* and growth opportunities to the many. It does require continuous effort, so it's a *lifetime* mission.

Why is social justice *my* life's mission? Because Jesus gave us a new *commandment*: "Love one another..."; He gave us a great *commission*: "Go...make disciples of all nations…"; and He also warned us (through the parables of *The Rich Man and Lazarus* (Lk. 16:19-31), and *The Last Judgment* (Mt. 25:31-46)) about the consequence of sins of *omission* – of not doing works of mercy.

How can I specifically accomplish this mission? Social justice work is often a battle against the wicked bent on protecting their own **w**ealth, **h**onor, **p**ower, and **p**leasure – *W-H-P-P* – items that enslave them and in turn oppress others. To win the battle, use these tactics on these entities:

1) *You* – you work to raise *your* interior life by detaching from personal WHPP addictions/obsessions; recasting them into a force *for* the common good: your wealth is diverted toward charity; your honor (celebrity) is used to draw to you people in need of evangelization; your power (talents) is channeled into political actions that advance peace and justice; and your pleasures (passions) naturally engage you in affairs of interest that may also aid humanity.

2) *Sinners* – you share with them Christ's Gospel and the (below) Spiritual Works of Mercy to alleviate their sin.

3) *Oppressed people* – you practice the (below) Corporal Works of Mercy and Jesus' new commandment to free from misery your brothers and sisters in Christ so that they themselves can pursue happiness – a life of goodness.

Your social justice vocation has great potential: you toil in it to transform yourself into a saint and transform sinners and the oppressed into social justice team members – fresh hands for building up the Body of Christ on Earth. Are you up for this adventure? To further the cause, encourage others and yourself to put into practice these powerful tools of virtue and truth:

✝ **Six Beatitudes** (for the battle against yourself): Blessed are the poor in spirit… (reject *wealth* as an end); Blessed are the meek… (reject *power* as an end); Blessed are they who mourn… (reduce selfish *pleasure*); Blessed are the merciful…; Blessed are the peacemakers…; Blessed are they who suffer persecution for justice' sake… (do the *right* thing, not the *popular* thing).

✝ **Five Corporal Works of Mercy** (to free the oppressed): Feed the hungry. Give shelter to the homeless. Give clothes to the naked. Give drink to the thirsty. Visit the imprisoned.

✝ **Subsidiarity principle** (when practiced, it aids the oppressed): it ensures that political decisions are being made at the lowest, practical level to help spark initiative and economic growth in individuals and small societies.

✝ **Three Spiritual Works of Mercy** (for the battle against sinners): Admonish the sinner. Instruct the ignorant. Counsel the doubtful.

✝ **The new Commandment** (for all to use in the fight for social justice): "…love one another. As I have loved you…" (Jn. 13:34)

But **who** can bear social justice toil? With a seafaring analogy in mind, let's see:

Within each of us is *goodness* and *truth*. Both are weak in (deck-bound, cowardly) souls who bow to wealth, worries, and pleasures. For others who run into rough seas of public resistance while going about a purposeful life: peer pressure may return them to the boat. But for those who partner with God in every moment and ask Him to impart to them wisdom, courage, and tenacity: they'll wade in and remain afloat over social justice duties and grow as pilgrims in a life of purpose. The moral: let go; let God. For God's grace *does* impart to a *willing* heart.

Author's note: A *pilgrim* can also spark goodness in others. I saw this when one charitable soul proposed creating a Gong Show to benefit the local homeless: many quickly and freely joined in and managed the show's production, video, and ad teams; one musician even auditioned and joined a college band just for the chance to plead (successfully) with trumpet players to come play in the show's pit band; other musicians cheerfully volunteered, too; and many (yearly) Gong show prize winners signed over their full winnings to the cause. Clearly then, to grow the seeds of goodness, it often just takes an agent of good and a local worthy cause; so bloom where you're planted! But caution: some will ignore, refuse, ridicule, despise, hassle or abuse you over your charitable efforts. Patience! This is where God's grace assists you in your journey to Heaven. Have these mantras in mind when floating in the deep: "Problems are my ticket chances to Heaven", and "Jesus, I tie my sufferings to yours on the cross." And be assured: while persisting in good works in the sea of Resistance, the Holy Spirit will temper your fears and doubts, causing you to become more vigorous and daring in your just aims. Your convictions will also awaken goodness in dormant hearts (just as early Christians' charity overwhelmed the Romans' hearts). So, get out of your lifeboat and heed Jesus' call to be His eyes, mouth, feet, hands, and ears on Earth. Be His witness and captain others to Him. It's *you* who can bear a baptism in Spirit – in swashbuckling good deeds for Him.

Baptized in Spirit – final words: Followers of Christ know that the goal is *to help myself and others get to Heaven* (with God's grace). So don't be silent in the face of evil. Step over the line and become a part of the (social justice) fellowship of the unashamed, armed with these banner statements:

Mission Statement ➜ "Help free sinners from their wickedness; defend the lowly and fatherless; render justice to the afflicted and needy. Rescue the lowly and poor; deliver them from the hand of the wicked." [Ps. 82: 3-4, enhanced].

Vision Statement ➜ "Those freed from sin and oppression have become the new builders of justice, peace, and the common good; joining other team members in holy acts on Earth and later as heirs to the heavenly Kingdom."

Be God's Witness:

"If anyone wishes to come after me, he must deny himself and take up his cross daily and follow me. For whoever wishes to save his life will lose it, but whoever loses his life for my sake will save it. What profit is there for one to gain the whole world yet lose or forfeit himself? Whoever is ashamed of me and of my words, the Son of Man will be ashamed of when he comes in his glory…" – Jesus [Luke 9:23-26]

"The world offers you comfort, you were not made for comfort, but for greatness." – Pope Benedict XVI

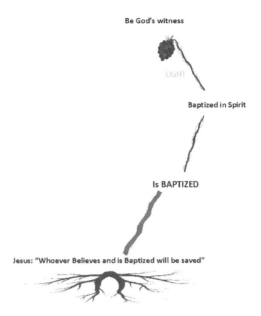

Be God's witness

LIGHT

Baptized in Spirit

Is BAPTIZED

Jesus: "Whoever Believes and is Baptized will be saved"

Being God's witness = Being Christ's **rebel**. That means it's you and God vs. the secular world and Satan. God is always with you, but He lets you be His voice, eyes, ears, hands, and feet. This can be trouble for you as your Christian deeds and words conflict with family, friends, and strangers who are pursuing their inheritance *now* through comfort, sin, and pleasure – as did the prodigal son.

Adopt rebel attitudes! All of us who are young-at-heart are to be bold and courageous when accosted by the world – like a ship's captain who breaks out into a galliard dance just prior to battle; or the Spartan commander who goes up against a foe outnumbering him 500 to 1. When an officer tells him that the enemy is so numerous that when they let fly their arrows, they block out the sun, the Spartan commander says, "good, then we shall have our fight in the shade!" Likewise, we are to be rebels for Jesus in defense of His name and teachings, even unto death. This means that you have something to die for. Do *you* have such a cause? One that makes you think that "Life shouldn't be a journey to the grave with the intention of arriving safely in a pretty and well-preserved body, but rather to skid in broadside in a cloud of smoke, thoroughly used up, totally worn out, and loudly proclaiming 'Wow! What a Ride!'" – Hunter S. Thompson

Being a rebel for Christ means being a martyr for God. And some martyrs may die, while the rest experience a hard life…So be it!

Being God's witness = Martyrdom. It's imitating Christ's life by picking up the *new* tree-of-life – your cross – and accepting any suffering, pain, or ridicule by it. Flip the crucifix over to the blank side, and that's *your* cross. As you carry it, know that Jesus travels with you. He has your back. Finally, know this: God does not promise to make you happy in *this* life, but in the *next*.

 Being God's Witness: *C-R-O-S-S* is the acronym (and **one of the 8 streets to Christ**) for witnessing – and each letter in *CROSS* is what God's witness *is* or *does*:

C: Corporal works of mercy (FSS CIDD) →

- The witness gives out food/shelter/clothing/drink; visits the imprisoned and sick; and buries the dead. *Translation*: They receive Jesus in the Eucharist, then go out and look for Him in the faces of the poor. Works of mercy are acts of social justice for those in the Body of Christ. And doers of mercy know that when one person in the Body is harmed or hurt in some way, it affects the whole Body.

- On hunger: Enter Norman Borlaug, a Christian. In the 1940s, he rejected the Dupont company's offer to double his salary and instead moved to Mexico to try to increase their wheat crop yields. He succeeded and saved one million people from starvation. He later went to India, Africa, and China, to increase their crop yields, often living in squalid conditions in war-torn and mosquito-infested areas. He could have made millions on his plant technologies, but instead chose to save a billion people from starvation.

- On homelessness: "To enter into the world of the homeless is to be barraged by sights, sounds, smells and struggles. It's to witness firsthand the brokenness in humanity in drug addiction, mental health sickness, and at times, crime. On the other hand, they're people just like you and me. Each homeless woman or man is a person, with an inherent dignity, made in the image of God. In their faces and bodies is Jesus. Sometimes it's a difficult experience, [but] I…feel…spiritually renewed in serving them." – Brian Kranick

How does God respond to these good works? Look to the Gospels. Only two miracles appear in all four Gospels: The Resurrection, and the multiplication of the loaves and fishes. Both are messages about how giving triggers exponentially good things. Jesus gives up His life so that billions may have a chance at eternal life, and a boy gives up his lunch so that God can feed thousands.

In the latter story, the crowd sits and expects Jesus to do something for them – all but the boy, who gives. Jesus takes this giving and multiplies it to feed 5,000, and more. **Moral:** God wants our lives modeled on charity, and when we do a good work, He responds by multiplying its goodness, exceeding expectations. The boy's sacrifice has been spoken about for 2,000 years and in all countries of the world.

R: Rebel ➜

- Christ's rebel is bold and not afraid to say they're Catholic. Rebels shun the vain use of God's name; aren't ashamed of Jesus; defend Him as the one, true God; admonish others when they're sinning; remind others to keep Sunday holy and as a day of rest; and remind others to be pro-life: *against* the use of contraceptives, abortion, and euthanasia (mercy killing).

- Rebels defend God and others like they defend friends and family members, through actions: they participate in pro-life events, or prayer groups at abortion clinics; they speak up when the media attacks Catholic Church teachings; they toil on social justice issues to help free the world's oppressed; they warn young people of secular society's desire to erase moral wrongs through a lullaby of pleasant-sounding *euphemisms*, such as "women's health care", "aid in dying", and "partners"; and, for the courageous, they peacefully challenge others at pro-choice or anti-Catholic events.

- Rebels recognize today's culture as destructive to human values, and one that doesn't require us to think. The culture expects us to just go along with the flow, don't ask questions, just enjoy yourself; just be a consumer, buying the latest toys and fashions. Rebels know that God cares more about them than the world does. God is driven by love for you, while the culture is driven by blind consumption. Be a rebel, reject the world's vision for your life and warn people about being consumed by it. Defend God, when appropriate, by saying this: **"I can't do that because my Faith tells me…"**

- Christ's followers warn others of spiritual deception: for example, they refute people claiming to be mediums and conjuring up the dead for a fee [necromancy]. Their message is never from God, but from 'spirit'; a spirit that never asks for prayers and whose messages are from alleged, deceased loved ones who're in a happy place. The medium is actually getting messages from impostures – demons – that lull the victim into thinking that everyone appears to be saved, so why follow Jesus, with His message to repent, pray to God, and go to Church? Recall: *"…Satan himself masquerades as an angel of light."* [2 Cor. 11:14]

Finally, rebels suffer greatly, being ridiculed, attacked, and hated for all the aforementioned acts. But they know that when you belong to Christ, His mission is now your mission.

O: Otherworldly ➔

- Those who belong to Christ first improve their *interior* life before going out to witness. They pursue Christ-like levels of patience…humility…love… obedience…virtue…and mercy. They know that God reads all thoughts. They behave as if this is their last day on Earth. Witnesses follow Jesus' advice that He gave to Sr. Faustina in 1938:

"Know that you are on a great stage where all Heaven and Earth are watching you."

- Otherworldly witnesses live by the four fluid Beatitudes:
  † Be poor in spirit   [shun **W**ealth as an end]
  † Suffer persecution for justice's sake [shun **H**onor]
  † Be meek   [shun **P**ower]
  † Mourn   [shun **P**leasure as an end]

  Shunning wealth, honor, power, and pleasure *(**WHPP**)* is rejecting the whip – the symbolic weapon by which you torture Jesus. This doesn't mean to ignore wealth or power if you plan to use them for the sake of others or to build up the Body of Christ on Earth. Do consider money not as your own, but that which is being managed for God. Likewise, pleasure through carefree timelessness may offer opportunities to help others or evangelize them. Jesus, instead, asks you to throw down your personal WHPP, pick up your Cross, and follow Him.

- Otherworldly witnesses live, love, and work *differently*.

  "If we look and act the same as the secular culture around us, then we can hardly be a witness to the throngs of people who are searching for something to fill that God-sized hole in their souls." – Fr. Bill Peckman

  The witness may wear a crucifix or Christian T-shirt (perhaps with printed saying, "My *PROC* to Heaven: **P**ray–**R**ead–**O**bey–**C**harity"), put Christian bumper stickers on their car, or place the Nativity Scene on the lawn. They may also say grace in public, and it won't be forgotten:

  I started work at Bell Labs in 1982. It was lunchtime in my very first work-day ever, when I was invited to the cafeteria by three experienced co-workers. We grabbed our lunch and sat down. Kim Donnelly made the sign of the cross and said grace while the rest of us looked on. I felt uncomfort-able to see such a display. What courage on her part, and a bold action that left a mark on me. It's 37 years since that occurred. I now say grace in public because of her. She knew how to be God's witness.

- An otherworldly witness doesn't react as neighbors do to news, entertain-ment, surprises, victories, defeats, and stresses. They don't perk up when hearing gossip, and don't value popular entertainments or celebrity fashions. Being short-tempered is not their reaction to struggles, humiliation, or con-tradictions. Finally, on a positive note: when they're victorious, they often deflect and do not gloat.

- Being a disciplined, generous, happy, loving Christian is irresistible to others who live for themselves with no meaning or purpose. This Christian way helped convert the early peoples to Christianity 2,000 years ago, and it will work today, too – because human nature hasn't changed.

- A true Christian is also revealed in stressful, tough times. It's here where you remain positive, calm, and loving. People will also notice and know that the character of Jesus is being formed in you. But how can you behave well under duress? By knowing that the God of the universe said this: "I am with you *always*, even to the end of the age." (emphasis added) [Matthew 28:20], and St. Paul said this: "Rejoice always… In all circumstances give thanks, for this is the will of God for you…" [1 Thessalonians 5:16–18]

- Living and loving *differently* is also evident in two major teachings in Jesus' Sermon on the Mount:

o **Love of enemy** [Matthew 5:44] ➔ "…love your enemies, and pray for those who persecute you." Loving your enemies by killing them with kindness does win them over, and I've seen it work. Another tactic to diminish your anger towards a perceived enemy is to pray for them this way: "Lord, forgive them, for they know not what they do." Finally, to chide us into trying to love our enemies, remember this: We're no better than evil people if we only love those who love us.

o **Turn the other cheek** [Matthew 5:39] ➔ At the moment a person does wrong to you…pause. Neither fight nor flee, instead, stand your ground and challenge them to a redo. Like in a game of chess: challenge them to make a better move – give them a chance to have a change of heart. Three examples:

1) Black Bishop, Desmond Tutu, approached a small bridge. From the other side came a known racist who told the bishop to "step aside, I don't make way for gorillas." Bishop Tutu stepped to the side, gestured for the man to proceed, and calmly replied, "I do."

2) Mother Teresa walked into a bakery and asked for some stale bread for a small, starving child in her arms. The baker spat in Mother Teresa's face. Without even wiping the spit off her cheek, she said, "Thanks for the gift. Now how about some bread for the child?"

3) I once cursed at my sister; she simply stood still and said, "That's not a nice thing to say." She made me realize that I had done a wrong thing to her.

Otherworldly final thoughts:

Become a saint in your life ➔ Pursue pure thoughts, words, and deeds; walk with God today and be a blessing to those you meet; be in a *state of grace* (actively in a relationship with Jesus and having no mortal sin on your soul). A saintly life's progression is shown later.

S: Suffering ➔

• It's when you take your cross off your shoulders, plant it in the ground, and then hang on it – next to Jesus, as did the Good Thief. It's the time to cry out, **"Lord, I suffer with you."** It's your Passion. Suffering humbles and strips you of comfort to make you more like Christ. This is when you're closest to Him – and when your progress to God is most productive. Suffering will occur for you and cost you friends or family, or result in physical or verbal force against you: when you admonish others, or remind them to keep Sunday holy, or speak out at a pro-choice rally for the unborn. Expect to be abandoned. But be at peace knowing that Jesus will stick up for you to the Father when the Judgment arrives. Know, too, that suffering is like a *death* that ironically gives you *life*.

- Suffering sometimes will lead to real death – martyrdom. Pope Francis told the story of a Muslim couple who were visited by terrorists. They saw the wife wearing a crucifix and ordered her to throw it on the ground. She refused, so they slit her throat. The husband witnessed her death and now wears a cross of suffering for the rest of his life. A question may come to mind: why did she risk her life when it could have been used for decades to serve the Lord? The answer is two-fold:
  1) She was martyred, so she gave up her grain-of-sand life and instantly gained the entire eternal beach.
  2) Her witness spouse now suffers on Earth but can use his life to inspire others to defeat evil.

- Remember the words of St. Paul: "I consider that the sufferings of this present time are as nothing compared with the glory to be revealed for us." [Romans 8:18] You may have to die for your Faith, but while here, at least *live* for it. And bring your kids up as martyrs, too. Not with death in mind for them, but in a life grounded in something that they're willing to die for: Christ and His Church.

- Some powerful words on suffering from saints:
  ✝ "If God sends you many sufferings, it is a sign that He has great plans for you and certainly wants to make you a saint." – St. Ignatius Loyola
  ✝ "Let all men know that grace comes after [suffering]…Let them know that…grace increase[s] as the struggles increase…This is the only true stairway to Heaven, and without the cross they can't find [the way] to Heaven." – Jesus [from the writings of Saint Rose of Lima]
  ✝ "Think yourself happy if you can exchange the agonizing pains of purgatory for sufferings in this world." – St. Francis Xavier
  ✝ "Christ tells us that if we want to join him, we shall travel the way he took. It's surely not right that the Son of God should go His way on the path of shame while [humans] walk the way of worldly honor. The disciple isn't above his teacher, nor the servant greater than his master." – St John of Avila

✟ "This, in short, is the difference between us and others who know not God, that in misfortune *they* complain and murmur, while the adversity does not call *us* away from the truth of virtue and faith, but strengthens us by its suffering." (Emphasis added) – St. Cyprian

✟ "One day, I saw two roads. One was broad, covered with… flowers, full of joy, music and all sorts of pleasures. People walked along it, dancing and enjoying themselves. They reached the end of the road [where] there was a horrible precipice; the abyss of hell. The souls fell blindly into it; as they walked, so they fell. And their numbers were so great that it's impossible to count them. (For a more graphic and scarier vision of hell, see the Appendix.) And I saw the other road…narrow and strewn with thorns and rocks; and the people who walked along it had tears in their eyes, and all kinds of suffering befell them. Some fell down, but stood up and went on. At the end of the road there was a magnificent garden filled with all sorts of happiness, and all these souls entered there. At the very first instant they forgot all their sufferings." (Condensed) – Diary of Saint Maria Faustina Kowalska, #153

S: Spiritual works of mercy (PACC FIB) ➜

• Pray for the living and the dead; Admonish [correct] sinners; Counsel the doubtful; Comfort the sorrowful; Forgive injuries; Instruct the ignorant; Bear wrongs patiently. On correcting sinners, this was written: If you don't warn others of their sins, then you will be held accountable. [Ez. 3:17-21] Also forgive in a spectacular way, perhaps like the Amish did in 2007, when they forgave the school shooter of their own kids: donating monies to the shooter's widow and children, and going to the killer's burial service.

Being God's Witness – Additional Things

CROSS FIRE: Lighting it for others to see

Jesus asked us to be perfect, like God the Father. That means we must pursue holiness. Holiness is attractive. Think about it: popularity fades, but saintliness is always remembered. Jesus also asked us to be the LIGHT of the world [Matthew 5:14-16]. This means that you must go out in public and do good deeds. Not as a chest-beater, brow-beater, or world-beater; but as a nothing – as a humble, lowly, servant. And your wooden *CROSS* is good tinder that combusts into LIGHT. It's lit by your good deeds of Corporal and Spiritual works of mercy, and by your rebel defense of God's good Name and Word. Your enflamed cross hopefully triggers a Divine fire in others. That's your duty as cross bearer ➔ God's witness, God's Martyr, God's LIGHT on Earth. So be it!

CROSS WALK: Carrying it while doing God's Will

Align yourself with God's will: "...whatever you do, do *everything* for the glory of God." (Emphasis added) [1 Corinthians 10:31] To discover God's plan for your life, ask Him: "What's the purpose of my life?" But while you're waiting for His answer, be at peace knowing that you're active in God's plan for your life and doing His will *whenever* you're using your resources to think/say/do something for God or neighbor. We all have passions, skills, and jobs. Use all three to do God's will. Examples:

1) Your passion is making dried flower arrangements. If you sell them and donate some of the profits to benefit others, your passion is being used to do God's will.
2) You have a job. If you help a co-worker or show patience with them, or you have a cheerful attitude while doing tough work, then you're using your job to do His will.
3) You have a skill. If you use it to freely instruct others or donate some of your skill's made wages to charity, that's doing God's will.
4) You rest and treat Sundays as a true holy day [Luke 23:56]. You also go to Confession when needed and try to obey God's Commandments. All these actions align with His will.

Moral: don't wait for the perfect life plan. Just use your passions, skills, and talents now to benefit humanity.

CROSS MULTIPLY: Use Social Media to multiply your good

In all CROSS-acronym *items*, use social media to increase a hundred-fold your giving, living, and good deeds. Think: "loaves and fishes" story.

WITNESSING: *This* You Can Do

Still need to be convinced? Then consider what these ordinary people did with their Faith witnessing:

- Mother Olga of the Sacred Heart saw four Iraqi wars in her 49 years. At 13 years old, her middle school was bombed, and she witnessed the death of teachers and students. At 16, she volunteered in her church because they had five to six funerals a day. At this time, she also saw a pregnant new bride – whose husband was deployed – come in to identify his corpse just by the remains of his lower body.

  Mother Olga walked miles to get water from a well, and her village had no electricity. She volunteered in a hospital that had only one baby incubator and saw grieving parents of babies who had died because the incubator was unavailable to them.

  She started a movement called Love Your Neighbor, where Muslims and Christians would beg for food, clothes and medicine for those left with a disability or homeless by war. She studied the Quran in order to build bridges between Christians and Muslims, so that these war-torn people could heal.

  She traveled to the USA to study, but then 9/11 (the World Trade Center disaster) occurred, so she returned to Iraq to care for both Iraqi people and U.S. troops. "I felt I was called to be that bridge," she said. She later returned to the USA to finish a Master's degree, and then she got cancer. She recovered, became a Roman Catholic, and was hired by the Archdiocese of Boston to serve in Boston University's campus ministry.

  Later, after the clergy sex abuse scandal and cover-up, she was asked to be a part of The Daughters of Mary of Nazareth, a private faith group. It focused on the corporal works of mercy, serving in hospitals, nursing homes, and parishes. Of her current life, she says, "Spiritually the Lord has entrusted me with the cross to raise this new community in the Archdiocese of Boston, the diocese that has suffered so much… I have said yes, not because I believe I have something to offer, but because I believe in following in the steps of the one [Mary] who said yes 2,000 years ago. She teaches me every day how to believe that there's nothing impossible for God."

- Moses. He wasn't a king, but God tasked him with going to the mighty Pharaoh of Egypt to demand that he release all his slaves. No one could ever convince a ruler to give up his human possessions (for who would make Pharaoh's bread, beer, and pyramids?) But Moses had faith that God would be with him, so he decided to attempt the impossible. His faith was the secret sauce that gave Moses an exodus to remember. And, if he had thought of it on the way out, his faith could have also moved a mountain into the [Red] Sea, too [Mark 11:23]

If Mother Olga could endure the carnage in four wars and Moses the suffering in 10 plagues, then we can surely do a few works of mercy for others, say grace in public, remind others not to use God's name in vain, and try to remove the addictive WHPP (Wealth, Honor, Power, Pleasure) from our own life. *Go.* Knock down the doors, get out there with confidence, and be a rebel for Christ. Long for the salvation of others, too, stopping at nothing to see others come to faith in Christ. Witnessing isn't something we do; it's who we are. Pray for opportunities to witness.

A Saintly Life's Progression

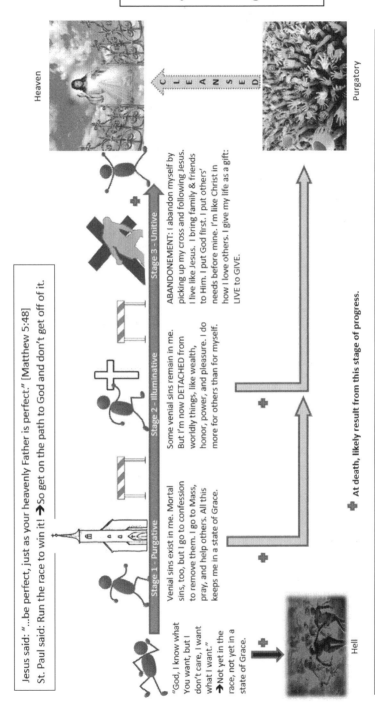

Heaven

Purgatory

C L E A N S E D

Jesus said: "...be perfect, just as your heavenly Father is perfect." [Matthew 5:48]
St. Paul said: Run the race to win it! → So get on the path to God and don't get off of it.

Stage 1 – Purgative

"God, I know what You want, but I don't care, I want what I want." → Not yet in the race, not yet in a state of Grace.

Venial sins exist in me. Mortal sins, too, but I go to confession to remove them. I go to Mass, pray, and help others. All this keeps me in a state of Grace.

Stage 2 – Illuminative

Some venial sins remain in me. But I'm now DETACHED from worldly things, like wealth, honor, power, and pleasure. I do more for others than for myself.

Stage 3 – Unitive

ABANDONEMENT: I abandon myself by picking up my cross and following Jesus. I live like Jesus. I bring family & friends to Him. I put God first. I put others' needs before mine. I'm like Christ in how I love others. I give my life as a gift: LIVE to GIVE.

Hell

✠ At death, likely result from this stage of progress.

✠

My life is a constant journey towards God. Each moral choice I make takes me a step closer to Him. My goal is to be happy forever with God, in Heaven, and bring family and friends with me. So I must strive to become holy and a saint in my lifetime, with God's help. And if I die in a state of Grace, whatever is left of my journey to God and Heaven is made up in Purgatory. SEEK GOD...PURSUE HEAVEN...WIN THE RACE.

Evangelize: "The harvest is abundant but the laborers are few…" – Jesus [Luke 10:2]

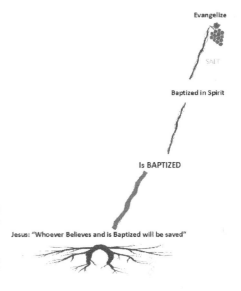

Jesus said this to His disciples prior to sending them out to evangelize. Later – after His ascension into Heaven, the disciples boldly went out with the message, "Christós Anésti! Christós Anésti!" [Christ has Risen!], and with the Good News: Jesus' death and resurrection gives you a path to Paradise; if you would just imitate Him by your life.

Today, too, Christians must go out to evangelize others. Proof? Jesus' Great Commission: "Go…make disciples of all nations, baptizing them in the name of the Father, and of the Son, and of the Holy Spirit, teaching them to observe all that I have commanded you. And behold, I am with you, *until the end of the world.*" (Emphasis added) [Matthew 28:19-20]

So, while Earth spins, we must go out to transform souls.

Evangelization is essentially a battle for souls. *You* can do battle – in small steps. Think of the first step a person might take to add exercise to their daily routine: they simply *stand* on a treadmill, then build on that success over the days ahead. Or, the first step a person may take to overcome laziness: they make their bed, a small feat that creates a small sense of pride and encourages them to do other little things that accumulate into a day of accomplishments.

What's the first small step for Christian evangelizers? Greet those you see with one question…

ASK ➜ 'How *are* you?'

Ask this while making eye contact, then truly listen to their response. For undoubtedly there will be someone out of many that day who seem melancholy or answer with a heavy heart; because all are fighting a great battle. For the heavy-hearted, here's your chance to be a Christian evangelizer. First you must build trust with them, so simply ask a follow-up question: 'No, really, how *ARE* you?', then *listen* again. And the *next day* follow-up with them. Subsequent visits will allow you to eventually gently share your Catholic faith and your own pursuit of a personal relationship with Jesus – all that enables you to live well and be happy.

What other things allow you to evangelize simply?

Be the EAR ➜ just listen to all who are weary and need rest.

Evangelizing can't be simpler: Ask others "How are you?" and let them verbally put their problems in your ear. Make listening to others your earthly occupation. I know a secretary who's the *EAR* for many women at work. She just lets them vent for a while and rarely interrupts them. Her listening skills and the frequency of drop-by visits to her prove that she's a pro listener and a human magnet for evangelizing others.

Be the HAND ➜ Help people with their problems.

Problems are God's *ticket chances* to Heaven and He hands them out daily. Just look at His design for human nutritional needs: we must eat daily, else we live in misery. Why not make human energy needs like those of ticks: just a meal once per year? Because then there would be no need to feed the hungry, interact with each other often, or slog through a 9-5 workday to support and feed the family. The world would also be filled with the complacent – those pursuing their next pleasure event, not their next meal. God, instead, made food a need – as opportunities for frequent interaction and aid to others. These *helping hand* occasions give us the chance to improve our own eternal lot.

Problems: those that don't kill us do make us stronger. But how do you motivate yourself to listen to and work on the problems of others that are often encased in stressful events? You do it by having this thought in mind:

Problems are *my* ticket chances to Heaven

Think of *problems* as God's way to get you to talk to Him – through prayer – as He tests your metal. Think of problems as your next chance to love your neighbor – a God directive. The very fact that God has placed a certain soul in your way is a sign that He wants you to do something for them; it's not by chance, it's been planned by God. All problems on which you toil well will move you one step closer to everlasting life. Yes, knowing that you're progressing toward a forever happiness gives you the needed energy to patiently toil over daily problems.

Be Salt to them ➔

In the Sermon on the Mount, Jesus commanded us to be salt. Salt preserves and stops decay; so we are asked to go out to help heal people by giving them the Good News and directing them on a saintlier path. Our mission is to give hope to those in despair, to help those in trouble, to spread and defend the Faith, and to not be ashamed of Jesus Christ. In evangelization terms, to *be salt* means to cause others to thirst for God. How best to do this?

✟ Get the Christian seeds and plant them first in *yourself*. Get to know the commands of God and all of Jesus' teachings. Volunteer in religious education classes. Read the Bible. Read the book in hand. Christ must be within you before you can bring Him to others. Openness to, and acceptance of, God's grace is necessary before going out to share His Good News.

✟ Make time to go out to plant. Try hard to simplify your own life to rid it of extra problems that take time from your day: minimize the distractions – but not attention to the children, for they are gifts from God and future workers for the human harvest. Try very hard to also build up your skills and talents through education. Education will improve your finances and will lead to more personal free time over the decades. A simpler, more financially secure existence will increase your chances of travelling out to plant the seeds of Christianity in others.

✟ Hoe an opening in others for the seed: God's Word. Do whatever it takes to start a conversation: wear a crucifix or Christian T-shirt; walk a dog, carry a rosary, or stroll a baby. Find an opportunity to let others know how you're involved with the Church. Also, get to know people's cultural/social/religious ways and get to know the modern mind, its habits, problems and desires. Further, ask people what they have heard about the Catholic religion and its Church. Memorize Bible verses, too, and invoke them where appropriate in any given situation.

Another icebreaker: electrical power outages. For these events lay bare some of the victims' pride and dignity making them ripe for a humble conversation with you, "the helper", about blessed electrons, and Who's the source of them all.

✟ Plant the seeds. Volunteer often. Encounter the poor *directly* in their poverty, addiction and hardship, and ask them their name; be a problem solver; attract others by your humble words like, "I don't know", or, "I'm not perfect"; do small things with great love; show great patience and listening skills; and interact with many people. Discuss the call to holiness; to becoming a saint in your lifetime, and the fact that it's not as hard as it sounds – it's accomplished with God, and in small steps.

But what are the *specific* Christian seeds to be planted in others?

Goal of an evangelizer ➜ Share a message of hope with others.

Here are sharable starter messages:

M1: ➜ "I can trust the God of the Bible. He says seek Me and you shall find Me. He says come unto Me all you who are weary and heavy laden and I will give you rest. I don't know anyone who has not been weary. This is a God who is approachable! Not only approachable but loving. He cares enough to forgive our wrongs. But He allows all to choose or deny Him. He forces no one to serve Him. This is a God I can serve." [Bruce Chowning]

M2: ➜ God loves you, God has a plan for your life, God wants you to be happy, and God would rather die than risk living in Paradise without you.

M3: ➜ Heaven is that which "no eye has seen, no ear has heard." To obtain it, do what pleases God: "Believe and be baptized to be saved." *Believe* includes obeying Him and turning from sin. And be at peace, for He forgives any sin that you're sorry for[4] – ask Moses the murderer, David the adulterer, Rahab the prostitute, or Peter the denier.

Here's a detailed message:

M4: ➜ God loves you and wants you to be happy in Heaven with Him. He's even preparing a room for you; with a view that no eye has ever seen! He knows that you're no match for temptation, sin, and Satan, so He gives you tools to help you find your way Home. For instance:

- The Bible, as your life's instruction manual
- The Church and Mass to make sense of the instructions
- The sacraments of Baptism, Reconciliation, and Eucharist to remove sins and make you more holy
- The Holy Spirit: your spiritual, internal, navigation system, and the Church's mission Guide

---

[4] Except one: Blaspheming against the Holy Spirit. For vital readings on this, see Mark 3:20-30, and Matthew 12:22-32.

To accept Heaven, you must use these tools and try often to imitate Christ's life. Jesus said this: 'Believe and be baptized to be saved.'

Believe means:

- Trust in God and all His Truths. The Nicene Creed lists beliefs, and trust in Him is proven through your daily prayers and Bible readings.
- Obey all God's commands: the 10 Commandments, the 5 Precepts of the Catholic Church, and Jesus' new commandment: "Love one another".

Baptized means:

- In water – through the sacrament of Baptism
- In Spirit ➔ go out and be a witness to God by defending the faith and loving your neighbor in word and deed (be Light); and bring others to God through words (be Salt). And when we sin: repent and go to Confession.

☩ Believe + Baptized =
Trust + **O**bey + [have an] **I**mmaculate-soul + **L**ight + **S**alt = **T-O-I-L-S**

The heavenly race is won by the Christian who **TOILS**

You are asked to "Love the Lord your God with all your heart, soul, mind, and strength." *With all your heart* means: put all your earthly desires below your desire to know, love, and serve God. *With all your soul* means: incorporate the Sacraments into your life, especially feeding and cleansing the soul through the Eucharist and Reconciliation. *With all your mind* means: know your Faith, Scriptures, what you believe and why, and have an answer for any Catholic question that comes your way. *With all your strength* means: have the courage to obey God when you sense He is calling you to do something.

Conclude the detailed message by showing them the MAP to HEAVEN.

Later, recommend to others to read key New Testament Bible texts, like these:

☩ Luke 1:46-55 – Canticle of Mary: her moment of supreme joy while pondering the coming birth
☩ Luke 2:8-14 – Birth of Jesus: humble shepherds out in the fields first hear the glorious news

✝ Matthew Chapters 5-7 – Sermon on the Mount: the apex collection of Jesus'
teachings

✝ John Chapter 6 – Bread of Life: the only time Jesus lost disciples; but then
Peter delivers his great faith reply

✝ Matthew 25:31-46 – Judgment of the Nations: will you be judged to be a
sheep or a goat?

✝ John's complete Gospel: likely the most accurate of them all. Recall, John
did take Mary into his home, and she likely shared much with him

Gently remind them of things that may lead to their destruction: a) being lukewarm, b) not being sorry and not asking for forgiveness or mercy, c) not doing
the Works of Mercy.

Also recommend a good Catholic book and invite the person to Mass with you.
Prior to Mass, you should review Ch. 3's *Catholic Mass Map* in anticipation of
your post-Mass talk with a new friend in faith. For those who respond to
evangelization, offer them the Church's Rite of Christian Initiation of Adults
(RCIA).

All of these *salting* efforts lead one to ask others the evangelizer's summit
question ➜

"How's your relationship with Christ?"

Then listen to their answer. Most will fumble it, for they will be humbled by
your soul-bearing question. But don't let them suffer for long: share your *own*
past of God-awful, meager faith – because all have had a humble faith beginning. Recall: "Christianity is one beggar telling another beggar where he found
bread." – D. T. Niles

Here's another powerful, but subtle, way to evangelize:

Be LIGHT:

Jesus commanded this of us. As an evangelizer, *being light* primarily means living
morally by following God's commands and teachings; being modest in thought,
word, deed, and even in dress; and actively pursuing opportunities to love your
neighbor. The hope is that your example will indirectly evangelize others to
experience a change of heart that results in their intense pursuit of God. Being
light means: "Preach the gospel at all times; use words if necessary."

One example of being light: be seen in public freely maintaining, fixing or clean-
ing things. Perhaps one day you go sweep the dirt off a basketball court. As

you're doing this, someone might be driving by, spot you, and say to them-selves, "Hmm, there's Anne again, volunteering. Perhaps I should start doing more, too." This is a conversion moment for the driver – because of Anne, who has performed an evangelization without even knowing it. But one thing's certain: Anne will have great joy when she later enters Heaven after her earthly imitation of Christ and sees all of the people that she indirectly evangelized. What a sight!

A thought may have just crossed your mind: maybe I can evangelize by just liv-ing an exemplary life – volunteering once in a while and assume that others will learn from my being? Nice thought, but we all need to try harder. For there's more joy in Heaven over one sinner who repents than over 99 righteous people who have no need. So, God leaps for joy when those who were lost are found through the efforts of a bold Christian evangelizer. Remember His Great Com-mission for you, Christian soldier. We need to go out and talk to people, with a goal of asking them the evangelizer's summit question: How's your relation-ship with Christ?

Another way of being light to others: Use mass media, booklets, door-to-door visits, and Catholic tracts and flyers left in conspicuous places to evangelize people. Heavily use the latest social media platforms such as Twitter, YouTube, Instagram, Facebook, and Snapchat to bring Jesus Christ to the masses.

You'll become an active evangelizer if you remember these exemplary human lives:

- Saul of Tarsus. He was a religious Jew – usually enough for living life well, but he knew that he could do much better. So, he traveled over 1,000 (pedes-trian) miles in 25 years to share the news on Jesus' teachings and Resurrec-tion. For this, he was stoned and dragged out of town (with the hutzpah to return and preach again); rod and rope whipped; shipwrecked; threatened by robbers; and likely beheaded.
- St. Teresa of Calcutta – Mother Teresa. She worked for decades in India amongst the poor of the world. She inspired others to go out and teach the Catholic way of charity. She was on TV, wrote books, and is one of the great-est imitators of Christ. Her work won her the Nobel Peace Prize.
- Bishop Robert Barron. The tireless, social media king of Catholic evangeliza-tion. He created the *Catholicism* DVD series, and uses Facebook, Twitter, and YouTube to bring millions to Christ. His simple explanations on Catholic topics – like the Beatitudes – inspired me to write this book.

Well done good and faithful servants! If they can do these things for Christ, then can't we simply ask one another, "How are you?" and be a hand and an ear on people's problems, share the Good News, and ask, "How's your relationship with Christ?"

Evangelization: Treading water with others

Back to Love's swimming pool: Whereas acts of love are hard, sacrificial dives into the pool of people's problems with refreshing effects, the act of evangelization is instead a subtle wade into the pool. You then encounter a person and their circle of woe not by chance but because God wills it. You don't just throw them a life-preserver; rather, you stay and tread water with them. Here, carefree timelessness establishes trust. For life is a string of daily problems, and your persistent acts of kindness towards another prove that you're with them *now*. Everyone appreciates that kind of support. Further, your help is not the usual one-and-done like so many charitable acts; you do not just donate to a GoFundMe cause, then move on. Evangelization is not hit-and-run, but sit-and-stay…and listen…until the person has recovered from their unfortunate event(s). This method leaves its mark and usually causes the victim to seek you out again out of trust and a curiosity on what makes you so different? This is the ideal time to share your Christian story and encourage the other – perhaps someone of little faith – to seek and find God like you have. For human change often occurs when people, *themselves*, decide to change – and this may be their moment!

Evangelization is most effective when it is summoned, not thrust on another; so, too, this may be your moment. After sharing your personal faith-based story, invite the person to Mass or Catholic gatherings to maintain their faith momentum. Here, all of your efforts gradually help move the person toward the edge of the pool where a human heart can be touched by its Maker. For you can only plant the Christian seeds in others to bring them near eternity's finish line. There, it's up to God to carry them over the line. But you have evangelized – you've done your part as God's tool. Be happy for it.

Yes, we must go out to evangelize others, but before we do…

We must evangelize our kids first because children are a gift from God [Psalm 127:3], and Ephesians 6:4 says, "…bring them [children] up in the discipline and instruction of the Lord." We must be our children's primary teachers of the Faith because we'll answer to God for how well we did this job. This is where this author fell down a bit, and I do regret it.

Evangelization and charity begin at home. The 'domestic church' is where mothers and fathers teach their children prayers and explain the meaning of the Christmas crib and the Crucifix. Parents also show their kids the meaning of unconditional love, the willingness to sacrifice for others, and how to be patient on tough tasks, making every day a reflection on how God loves *us*. Taking kids on religious trips, donating to the needy, participating in food drives, praying the rosary as a family, and doing Bible study all give witness to faith in Jesus and create family traditions that children appreciate. Traditions are the family binding agent and lead to more family happiness – important because an unhappy home was cited as the cause for 52% of Catholics leaving the Faith. (Parental note: Don't abandon your home to advance your career at the expense of raising your children). Faith abandonment has also been linked to fathers who didn't take the lead in religious matters and Mass attendance while their kids were growing up. A 1994 Swiss study found that Mass attendance by fathers early on was key to children's later attendance: 74% of children later in life at least irregularly attended Mass if dad had regularly attended when they were young. Attendance for kids dropped to 59% when their young father was an irregular Mass attendee, and to 37% if a father hadn't gone to Mass at all. Fathers must take the religious lead while their children are with them!

The Evangelizer's Toolkit

Evangelizers help bring others to everlasting life. How's that for your life's purpose? An evangelizer's goals are: help others turn away from sin and escape eternal death by turning back to God. So, an evangelizer **H-E-A-L-S** (an acronym, and **one of the 8 streets to Christ**). Carry these tools in life:

> **H**: lend a *hand* on others' problems.
> **E**: lend a patient *ear* on others' issues.
> **A**: *Ask* & *Acknowledge*. Ask two questions: "How are you?"; then later, "How's your relationship with Christ?" *Acknowledge others*: A channel of communication for evangelizing others can be opened by: a) giving others appropriate, positive feedback (a charity of words), or, b) asking their opinion on a matter. Both will build their trust and willingness to dialogue with you. Talks will follow.
> **L**: Be *light* by living your Christian life in view of others to trigger in them this thought: "Maybe I should do more?"
> **S**: Be *salt*; imparting Christian ideas on others so that they too then thirst for a relationship with Jesus.

Also carry the following tools of the mind while out gathering souls for Christ.

The evangelizer's motto: '…Christ has no body now but yours, no hands, no feet on Earth but yours.' – St. Teresa of Avila poem

And these thoughts:

"Bring the Kingdom of God to whatever place you're entering." – Anonymous

"People only listen to an excited speaker." – Aristotle.

"If you had the cure to cancer, wouldn't you share it? You have the cure to death, so get out there and share it." – Kirk Cameron

"The world offers you comfort, you were not made for comfort, but for greatness." – Pope Benedict XVI

More help? Go to the St. Paul Evangelization Society for this master list of ideas for evangelizing others: https://www.spesinchrist.com/featured/99-effective-ways-evangelize-catholic/

Final thoughts on Evangelization:

You don't realize the *will power* for evangelizing others given to you by the Holy Spirit at Confirmation. I witnessed this power once, in an unlikely place; in a handball game with a friend, Michael Salvarezza:

We were very competitive teenagers in the 1970s. Both hated to lose – so we were big babies. We often played handball against a wall. Mike was quick, but I was ambidextrous. In one instance, I had won the last 10 games in a row – yay for me! On the final point of that 10th game – a resounding 21-11 win – Mike felt embarrassed by another bad loss and became angry and vowed to win the next game. I saw the rage emerge in him like at no other time, so I – the other big baby – became even more determined to heel the animal. The next game was tornadic with grunts and howls, sweat and semi-dislocated arms contacting the ball. The end-game score: 21-8. He *crushed* me. This was absolute, unleased, human *will*. It's a story I had hoped to tell, and now, 44 years later, it is in print. Mike had tapped into the unknown power within – that which we all have. Pray for this power when you plan *to go out* as Christ's soldier.

Active evangelization is God's plan for every Catholic. *You can do this.*

The Final Approach ➔
The pursuit of eternal happiness: a road too narrow?

Jesus Christ – the King of the Universe – told us how to get to Heaven: Mark 16:16. The earlier presented *Map to Heaven* was a satellite view. We then descended into vine paths, each summarized in the *Map to Heaven – Aerial View* below. This map is summarized by the phrase: A Christian who **TOILS** wins Heaven. That is, **T**RUST in God; **O**BEY His commands; have an IMMACULATE soul – obtained through Baptism and Divine Mercy Sunday; be **L**IGHT as God's Witness; and be **S**ALT by evangelizing others.

Your lifetime toils produce vine-terminal fruits – displayed here as acronyms and symbols:

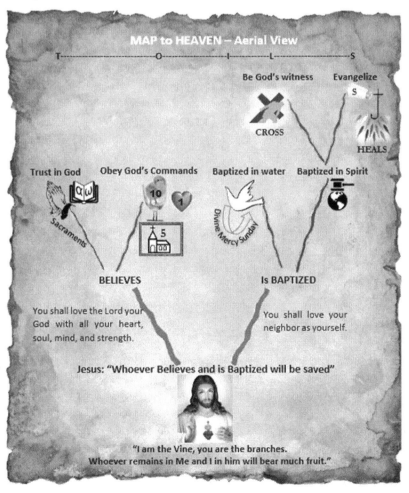

✝ *Trust in God* (and His truths): Prayer, Bible reading, and partaking of the sacraments are its fruits. All comprise the 2-way communication with Jesus and fulfill your personal relationship with Him.

✝ *Obey God's Commands*: Jesus said, "If you love me, you will obey my commandments." [John 14:15] Each Person in the Holy Trinity contributes a commandment set:

  o [God the Father's] 10 Commandments, with acronym *GLASS CHICK*: **G**oods – don't covet them; **L**ie – no false witness against thy neighbor; no **A**dultery; **S**abbath – keep it holy; don't **S**teal; don't **C**ovet thy neighbor's wife; **H**onor father and mother; **I**dols – no strange gods; **C**ursing – don't take God's name in vain; don't **K**ill.

  o Jesus' one new commandment: *Love one another.*

  o [Holy Spirit inspired] 5 Precepts of the Catholic Church with acronym *FRAME*: Take care of the Church's **F**inancial needs; yearly participate in the **R**econciliation sacrament; **A**bstain from meat and fast on appointed Lenten days; always go to **M**ass on Sundays and Holy Days; yearly receive the **E**ucharistic sacrament [Holy Communion].

✝ *Baptized in Water*: This produces an immaculate soul and makes you a child of God and therefore an heir! Christ also gives you an opportunity, yearly, to be cleansed of all sins *and punishments* on Divine Mercy Sunday. It is a Divine gift, for each year's sins and potentially imperfect confessions and penances are completely forgiven, and you are reborn into a state of grace.

✝ *Be God's Witness*: A sacrament of Confirmation objective. The *CROSS* acronym tells us how to shine our light as witnesses – martyrs – for Jesus:

  o Do **C**orporal Works of Mercy; be a **R**ebel for Christ – defending His name and teachings; be **O**therworldly by improving your *interior* life and then projecting it outward; accept **S**uffering as a path to Paradise; and do **S**piritual Works of Mercy.

✝ *Evangelize*: Another sacrament of Confirmation objective. An evangelizer *HEALS* – an acronym that defines the steps to be taken to help others avoid sin and become thirsty for God:

  o Lend a **H**and on others' problems; lend an **E**ar to problems; **A**sk: "How are you?", and "How's your relationship with Christ?"; and **A**cknowledge others' efforts in order to build trust; **L**ight – be an example of holiness as you go about your business; **S**alt – instruct the ignorant on Catholicism.

The fruit of your evangelizing efforts: leading others to God.

This *Map to Heaven – Aerial View* should make sense to your mind but *must* move to your heart. This trek requires hands, as in hands-on *good works*: those necessary for salvation. So, a Christian wins the race to Heaven via head-to-hands-to-heart, then outward – a three-legged event that builds up the Kingdom of God on Earth while cultivating good in your *soul*. And, your good works towards others are *your* duty. Their execution fulfills God's unique plan for your life.

Questions: Is your earthly prep and trek towards Paradise a road too narrow, a road too far? Is the toil too much to bear? These questions will help you decide:

1. Is your current life worth living? If yes, then so too is a ***forever life*** of love, health, safety, joy and peace.
2. Identify the happiest moment in your life. Is it something you'd like to re-visit? Is it something you'd like to experience often, at will? If yes, then ***eternal life*** would appeal to you, too.
3. Have you ever broken a bad habit? Have you ever formed a good habit? If yes to either, then you possess a ***will***.
4. Is there a moment in your life when you chose to leave your comfort zone to either save someone or say or do something of benefit to another? If yes, then you possess ***courage***.
5. Do you appreciate beautiful things (landscapes, music, human beings)? If yes, then you would also appreciate the beauty in that which "no eye has seen; no ear has heard".

Life is not always fair, but it is still worth living. We all have that one happy moment that we'd dearly like to *feel* again, especially if it involves a young child running to us. *Will* and *Courage* have, at times, been our guides in life. We have also seen beauty that has stolen our breath and long for beauty to rob us again. My friend, this book's prep and sprint to Heaven *is doable* based on your existing talents, character, and inner strength. Jesus knows this, so He said, "Take my yoke upon you and learn from me, for I am meek and humble of heart; and you will find rest for yourselves. For my yoke is easy, and my burden light." [Matthew 11:29-30]

The human being who possesses will, courage, and is *convinced* of the mission, cannot fail. An example of a life well-lived was that of President George Herbert Walker Bush. He postponed college to enlist in the Navy on his 18th birthday, became the youngest World War II Navy pilot, and risked his life flying missions over the Pacific Ocean. He later served for decades in high-ranking positions in the U.S. government, and, as Vice President, once led a top-secret mission into the jungle of El Salvador to meet and deliver a warning to armed and evil Salvadoran military commanders. Later in life, Bush always stressed service to others, volunteered often, sponsored children overseas, and was part of the Points of Light Foundation.

On November 30, 2018, President George Herbert Walker Bush, just hours before his death, was visited by his former Secretary of State, James Baker, with whom he had traveled often during the Presidential years. Upon seeing Baker, Bush grew alert, recalled their past, usual, business banter, and now said: "Bake, where are we going?", to which James Baker replied, "[Chief], we're going to Heaven" …"Good, that's where I want to go," Bush said. Hours later, President Bush died.

At the end of *our* lives, let's hope that our conversation with God goes the same way.

But what happens to those who don't know of the Gospel of Jesus Christ – can they be saved?

The Catechism of the Catholic Church, Reference# 1260, answers this way: "Since Christ died for all, and since all men are in fact called to one and the same destiny, which is divine, we must hold that the Holy Spirit offers to all the possibility of being made partakers, in a way known to God, of the Paschal mystery (Passion, death, and Resurrection of Jesus Christ). Every man who is ignorant of the Gospel of Christ and of his Church, but seeks the truth and does the will of God in accordance with his understanding of it, can be saved. It may be supposed that such persons would have desired Baptism explicitly if they had known its necessity."
* *

The following *Supernatural Designs* should convince you to take the right path toward Heaven. Just keep your eyes on the forever prize and use all 365 yearly ticket chances – and God's help – to try to win it. With so many daily opportunities, it's not *can* you do this, it's **what are you waiting for?** Life is not guaranteed, so don now the light-weight yoke and journey with your Guide.

You are *built* for happiness

 Your collective years of *effort* and *sacrifice* are short: 99 years or fewer

 You experience two kinds of happiness in life (as follows)

FROWN   SMILE

Examples:	Examples:
Sin	Study, education
Pleasure events	Skills development
Carefree timelessness	Exercise
	Virtues development
	Love of neighbor

FROWN-shaped happiness is like fireworks: quick, short-lived, Me-centered, addictive – *Oooh…Aaah* happiness. It is the kind that Jesus says passes away and is of little value – that which moth and rust destroy. To be satisfied here, you must often pursue pleasure – a poor substitute for happiness. But there's one beacon in FROWN happiness: *carefree timelessness*, when you stop and connect with others, strengthening relationships and building feelings of trust. Carefree timelessness is that wade-in-the-pool setup for evangelization: when you slowly, patiently, get a chance to convince people to pursue a more fulfilling happiness – in the SMILE arena – by saying, 'Go play over there.'

SMILE-shaped happiness is like night-sky stars: steady and sustained. Who doesn't want sustained happiness that leads to inner peace? SMILE happiness is associated with godly matters and virtues – such as discipline, courage, hard work, love, humility, patience, and perseverance – producing things that don't pass away. Jesus said that you'll be happy as soon as you move from *your* will and need for personal pleasures to a humble dependence and confidence in God. An aspiring saint plays long and hard in this SMILE arena, where dedication to its activities produces a *steady-state* of happiness called *JOY*.

SMILE happiness is OTHER-centered and charitable. Working in this arena makes you *like* a night star: where both your's and its light continue through time even after both of you have expired. Visible star light is centuries old, and so, too, can be your light, if you affect the young while on Earth thereby continuing your good *through* the generations. Consider this: if you truly affect two young people in your lifetime, and they then do the same in theirs, etc., in less than a millennium (33 generations), the world of 8 billion people will be pursuing holiness, resulting in a Heaven on Earth. Why not dream big?!

 You accept the prize of Paradise by traveling onboard the SMILE train. Being a passenger here proves that you've learned how to love, are putting random acts of kindness into action, are a saint in the making, and are progressing towards Heaven. Stay on board!

 You have **consciousness**. It's supernatural because science can't explain it.

 You're more than just a sloshy brain and beating heart: you have a ***soul***. It allows you to know right from wrong; to love; and to know truth, beauty, and goodness. The soul's existence proves that you have a spirit that's independent of the body. The soul is then evidence of an existing eternity.

 Overwhelming evidence for God is also evidence of an eternity.

Before we land, let's revisit this book's introductory thoughts on Stop-Then-Connect, where you treat Earth as the stopover, *not* the Paradise destination. Your earthly stopover and connecting flight have two steps:

1) Gather and trust the supplies given to you by God.

2) Work on pleasing God.

Let's explore both:

1) Gather and trust the supplies➜
God gives you everything to equip you for the upcoming travel:

✝ The Bible (God-inspired): life's instruction manual and map.

✝ The Church (with the Holy Spirit as its Guide): interpreter of the Bible, as well as guide on faith, morals, and charity.

✝ Your conscience, which is God's law written on your heart.

✝ Holy Spirit: He lives in you and interprets the heartfelt law; and enacts pangs of conscience when needed.

✝ Mary: a gift to us all when Jesus, from the cross, said to apostle John, "Behold, your mother." [John 19:27] Mary is also an end-of-life Advocate for you when Jesus comes to judge you.

✝ Rosary: the machine-gun belt of prayers that are shots at Satan. Each said prayer helps lessen his hold on you.

✝ Jesus' Crucifixion and Resurrection: a death for His friends to bury their sins; a Resurrection so that they may have a chance at everlasting life.

✝ The Mass: Contains Jesus' teachings and is a remembrance of His sacrifice on the cross for you; you also consume Jesus in the Eucharist in order to have life within you [John 6].

✝ Baptism, Divine Mercy Sunday, the Reconciliation sacrament – all from Jesus: used to remove your sins and restore your state of grace.

✝ The saints: your role models and spiritual all-stars that demonstrate how to get to Heaven.

✝ Your guardian angel: a guard and guide on the path to Heaven.

✝ Your cross: God's life plan for you. You execute the plan to prove your love for Him.

✝ Jesus: Your personal Guide Who daily walks with you.

How can you miss your paradise destination with all of these supplies in hand? God gives you supplies to aid your earthly journey because He later wants you *with* Him. *God wants to be found, by you.* Make no mistake: your life is a love story between God and you.

2) Work on pleasing God – described in a '*PL³S³ME*' [please Me] math acronym:

✝ Stop to **P**ray, which connects you with God.
✝ **L**ove a neighbor; **L**ove God by obeying His commands; be **L**ight to others through your exemplary life. All 3 *L's* connect you with God and people.
✝ **S**eek God through the evidence for Him; partake of the **S**acraments; and be **S**alt to others. All 3 *S's* connect you with God and others, strengthen your relationships, and build trust.
✝ **S**top what you're doing and go to **M**ass, to connect with Jesus through the **E**ucharist.

Summary: "Try to learn what is pleasing to the Lord" [Eph. 5:10] – then do it.

The Landing

Is eternal happiness worth it? …after a sand-grain life, is the move to a whole blissful beach worth it? Decide: in your lifetime, will you be a sap for Satan or a rebel for Christ? If your *head* says 'yes' to God, but your *heart* not quite yet, at least postpone judgment until you visit the following neighborhood…

We now move from the aerial map to the street map. Ahead is the (acronym-laden) **Street Map to Heaven** with its 8 streets. These are the streets of Mark 16:16. Start your journey on *any* block, visit each often, and create well-worn paths throughout. You must labor on this earthly course. Walking it like a tourist won't win an end crown of righteousness at its finish line. Matthew Kelly comments on the Christian street life: "There will be fabulous joy in the journey, as well as heart-wrenching pain. Anyone who offers you an easy path is to be mistrusted. Life is difficult and messy; there is no point trying to mask that or pretend otherwise. But every situation you encounter is in need of one thing: a holy moment."

You can create *holy moments* on each street tile in the map ahead. Scatter holy moments all over this neighborhood. But what's really happening on these 8 streets? Just the crux of this book, the purpose of your life, the *PROC* in action, the trek to obey God's summit commands, and the journey to Heaven:

You have entered into a personal relationship with Jesus.

Bishop Donald J. Hying describes the relationship this way: "He [Jesus] wants us to call on His mighty power, enjoy the intimacy of His presence through the sacraments, hear His gentle voice in the Word, and discover the beauty of His face in those around us."

Life will now be much more exciting. Don't want this? Then curl up with your unopened heavenly gift, take no risks, and count down your life clock – The End. Else, pick up your *tree of life* so that your worldly battle will be in the shade of Christ, and break into a galliard dance knowing your Brother has your back! What's in this brotherly, friendly relationship? All the usual, and more:

1) **You meet Jesus**: often, in Eucharistic Adoration (He is present in consecrated Host(s) in the tabernacle if its candle is lit).

2) **You talk with Jesus**: often and throughout the day, through prayer *to Him* about your business, your plans, your troubles, your fears and concerns – you pray confidently and frankly; and you listen to Him speak *to you* through private Bible readings and the Mass's Gospel readings.

3) **You receive Jesus**: in the most intimate way, by eating His flesh and drinking His blood in the Holy Eucharist during Mass.

4) **You ask Jesus for forgiveness**: through the yearly Feast of the Divine Mercy and the sacrament of Reconciliation.

5) **You defend Jesus**: as a Christian rebel. You say grace in public, defend His name, and defend His Church and its teachings. All is done with Jesus' saying in mind: "Everyone who acknowledges Me before others I will acknowledge before my heavenly Father." [Mt. 10:32]

6) **You suffer with Jesus**: by tying all your sufferings to His on the cross. You also practice *empathy* and *compassion* toward others.

7) **You help Jesus**: by seeing His face in people, you perform acts of love towards your neighbor. God's ministry for you is in here.

You can more easily do the following if a personal relationship with Jesus already exists:

8) **You run with Jesus**: by practicing virtues and obeying God's commandments. You remain in a state of grace, with no mortal sins of commission or omission on your soul.

9) **You introduce Jesus to others**: by sharing your Catholic faith.

So what does Jesus really mean by, "Whoever Believes and is Baptized will be saved"? (Mark 16:16) He wants you to enter into an intimate, life-saving relationship with Him.

So off you go. To the race's starting blocks. Commit these streets to memory. Commit your time, talent and treasure to this journey. Then, take great hope in knowing that your life of loving toil on these narrow 8 blocks will lead to a joyful relationship and eternity with Christ. For through His death and Resurrection, He has already paid for your ticket on the connecting flight to Paradise. And through your executed holy moments, you have *accepted* the ticket and its boarding pass...well done.

Become a street-wise saint in your lifetime. That is, if eternal happiness is your thing. ➔ ➔ ➔

Street Map to Heaven

"...I am going to prepare a place for you.." (Jn. 14:2)

Trust in God:
† 1 God in 3 Persons(Father;Son;Holy Spirit) = Holy Trinity
† Jesus died and rose from the dead - for me
† Jesus is truly in the consecrated Host = Eucharist
† Jesus made the Church, so I must follow *all* its teachings
† The Holy Spirit dwells within me and aids my conscience
† Jesus will come again to judge my love of God&neighbor
† Jesus walks with me daily and always

Evidence for God:
† Jesus' Resurrection
† Our Lady of Fatima
† The Shroud of Turin
† The Cloak of Guadalupe
† Our Lady of Lourdes
† Eucharistic Miracle: Lanciano
† Levitation
† Incorruptible Bodies
† Bilocation
† Reading Hearts
† Stigmata
† Eucharistic Miracle: Sokolka
† The Big Bang
† Christianity
† Human Consciousness
† Limpias Crucifix Miracle
† Eucharist-only survival
† Universal Physical Constants
† Face/finger/foot print DNA

† 4 Enzymes make cells' DNA
† Universe's Math Equations
† The Conscience & the Soul
† Dying: Everybody does it
† Earth: by Design or chance?
† Earth's pharmacy

Faith Park

Agape Pool

Crossword layout (across/down letters):
PACC - FIB / BAPTISM / CROSS / HEALS / FRAME / TOILS / GLASS - CHICK / LOVE / FSS CIDD

TOILS ► A summary acronym on the *Street Map to Heaven*: **T**rust (in God), **O**bey (commandments), **I**mmaculate soul (Baptism/Divine Mercy Sunday), be **L**ight (God's witness), be **S**alt (evangelize). TOILS in 2 ways: 1► PROC for Heaven: 'Pray–Read–Obey–Charity' 2► Phrase: 'A Christian who TOILS wins Heaven.'

ATYOS ► If I start my prayers with, 'God, have mercy on me, a sinner', God likely replies with, 'At your service...at yo service.' **ATYOS** stands for types of prayers to God: prayer of **A**doration, of **T**hanksgiving, prayer for **Y**ou, prayer for **O**thers; and added **S**ilence, too, to just be in the presence of God. **1**

LOVE ► Jesus' new commandment: Love one another. The *Agape Pool* lists outcomes for my acts of love: Humility (I'm ridiculed, embarrased, or laughed at); Sacrifice (I give up time or treasure that could instead have been used on me); Suffering; Pain; even death. My dive into the Agape pool is hard, but it refreshes others. **2**

FRAME ► Acronym for: 5 Precepts of Jesus' Catholic Church. I must follow these: Take care of the Church's **F**inancial needs; Yearly do the **R**econciliation Sacrament; **A**bstain from meat & fast on appointed Lenten days; Always go to **M**ass on Sundays & Holy Days; Yearly do the **E**ucharistic Sacrament. **3**

GLASS CHICK ► Acronym for 10 Commandments ► **G**oods - don't covet them; **L**ie - no false witness against my neighbor; No **A**dultery; **S**abbath - keep it holy; Don't **S**teal; Don't **C**ovet my neighbor's wife; **H**onor father & mother; **I**dols - no strange gods; **C**ursing - don't take God's name in vain; Don't **K**ill. **4**

CROSS ► relates to *Being God's Witness*: I need to carry my cross through life, defend God's name and teachings, behave unlike the secular world, and love my neighbor. **CROSS** means: do **C**orporal mercies; be a **R**ebel for Christ; be **O**therworldly; accept **S**uffering as a path to God; do **S**piritual mercies. **5**

HEALS ► Acronym for evangelizing others, where evangelization HEALS them. Lend a **H**and to others; Be an **E**ar to people's problems; **A**sk 'How are you?' & 'How's your relationship with Christ?', and Acknowledge others' efforts; Be **L**ight - let my life be an example to people; Be **S**alt - talk to others about God and make them thirst for Him. **6**

BAPTISM ► The Sacrament that creates an Immaculate soul. And Divine Mercy Sunday (2nd Sunday of Easter) is like a 2nd Baptism. For on or near it, if I have mercy in my heart towards others, and partake in the Sacraments of Reconciliation & Eucharist, then all my sins *and their punishments* are forgiven by Jesus. **7**

CORPORAL MERCIES ► Shining my light as God's witness means love-of-neighbor thru these 7 mercies in acronym: **FSS CIDD** (a corporal babysits a fussy kid): Give **F**ood; Give **S**helter; The **S**ick - visit them; Give **C**lothing; The **I**mprisoned - visit them; Give **D**rink; The **D**ead - bury them. **8**

SPIRITUAL MERCIES ► Love-of-neighbor mercies, too - acronym **PACC FIB** (the Spirit doesn't lie; the Spirit doesn't pack fibs): **P**ray for the living & the dead; **A**dmonish sinners; **C**ounsel the doubtful; **C**omfort the sorrowful; **F**orgive all injuries; **I**nstruct the ignorant; **B**ear wrongs patiently.

The goal of life on Earth:
☦ Help myself and others get to Heaven (with God's assistance).
☦ Ticket to Heaven? ► Learn how to love and put it into action.
☦ How do I love? ► By *running* these streets.

Live-bys:
☦ Have a relationship with Jesus, follow God's commands, and love my neighbor.
☦ Be merciful and I'll be shown mercy by God.
☦ Don't judge, and I won't be judged.
☦ Forgive, and I will be forgiven.
☦ I think and behave knowing that Jesus is *always* by my side.

Appendix A – Glossary

Christian term/phrase...	Meaning...
Alleluia/Halleluiah	Praise the Lord! or 'Praise Yahweh' ('uia' /'uiah' endings are short for 'Yahweh', a name for God).
Amen	Truth! It also means 'so be it!' And it means 'truly' when Jesus said, "Amen, amen, I say to you..."
...and with your Spirit	We acknowledge that the priest is standing in for Jesus, that the *Spirit* is Jesus.
apostolic	Created by the apostles and handed down to the Bishops, who dictate what we follow in the Church.
begotten	born, not made out of thin air.
blessed →	1) sacred <the Blessed Sacrament>; 2) worthy of worship <the Blessed Trinity>; 3) happy/content <I'm blessed>.
bless →	1) favor and protect (us and our food) <Bless us, Oh Lord, and these thy gifts>; 2) to protect from evil <Bless you!>; 3) to make the sign of the cross over: <The Pope came to bless the crowd>.
catholic	universal – because the Catholic Church welcomes and is composed of all who believe in Christ.
Christ	The Anointed One. And, it means the Messiah, the deliverer of the Jewish people.
consubstantial	of one and the same substance → Jesus is consubstantial with the Father and Holy Spirit: 1 God, 3 Persons.
creed	A statement of belief by a religious group. Christians have 2 creeds: Apostles Creed, and Nicene Creed.
Emmanuel/Immanuel	God is with us. And it means Jesus Christ, especially as the Messiah.
Eucharist	Thanksgiving; the sacrament of Holy Communion; the sacrifice of the Mass; the Lord's Supper.
Gospel	The *Good News*; the teachings of Jesus.
grace →	Getting what we DON'T deserve. Grace is *favor*, in 2 flavors: **Sanctifying grace** is *interior* grace, which dwells in the soul and makes it holy. We receive it thru sacraments. When you die, you must be in a state of grace (in a relationship with God, with no serious sin on your soul) to be heaven-bound. **Actual grace** is like a nudge from God. It's *external* grace, prodding us to deepen our relationship with Him. All receive this grace when it is needed, but we have to accept it for it to work.
Compared to: justice →	Getting what we DO deserve.
mercy →	Not getting what we DO deserve. You're pardoned, you don't receive justice, you're let off the hook.

Christian term/phrase...	Meaning...
Hail, Holy Queen, Mother of Mercy...	Hail, Holy Queen, Mother of Jesus... (because Mercy is capitalized)
Our life, our sweetness, ...our hope. To thee...we cry...weeping in...tears.	These lines and references to *mercy* and *clement*[=mercy] say this: we depend on Mary now and at our death to show us mercy thru her prayer to God, and thru her intercession on our behalf with Jesus.
He [Jesus] descended into hell...	[In Apostles Creed]: Scripture used the term *hell* to mean the abode of the dead. Jesus, as Savior, descended into this hell, proclaiming the Good News only to the [non-damned] spirits imprisoned there.
holy	saintly; godly; pure in thought, word, and deed; dedicated or devoted to the service of God
homily	A sermon, typically explaining the meaning of the day's Gospel reading
Hosanna	A shout of praise → "Hosanna in the Highest" might mean "Rejoice in the Highest"
incarnate	embodied in flesh → "...incarnate of the Virgin Mary" means "...a human body in the Virgin Mary"
INRI	Jesus of Nazareth, the King of the Jews. Latin phrase where 'I' is an English 'J', and 'R' is 'Rex' for King.
Jesus	God saves
Kyrie eleison, Christe eleison	"Lord, have mercy", "Christ have mercy"
Lamb of God	Jesus → in reference to Him, who was sacrificed for us on the cross and sent to the slaughter like a lamb
liturgy	public worship
...of all things visible and invisible.	The Father is the creator of the visible (physical) world, and the invisible world of the angels.
one, holy, catholic, apostolic Church	One church/one body, holy because it was started by Jesus, catholic (universal, welcoming all), and handed down from the apostles to the Bishops through the generations.
penitent	Feeling sorry for sin or wrongdoing; repentant; contrite. And: a Roman Catholic who confesses sins and does penance.
(1) sacristy, (2) sanctuary	(1) Room in the back of the church where sacred vessels and vestments (outfits) are kept. (2) Area around the altar.
Sin types: venial →	Less serious sins that offend or wound but do *not* separate you from God.
mortal/grave →	Serious sins that are done deliberately and with full knowledge that they're sins. Example: deliberately breaking one of the 10 Commandments, with this attitude: "God, I know what you want, but I don't care, I want what I want."
Tabernacle	The decorated box sitting on a high altar (traditionally near a red lamp) in church. Jesus truly resides in the tabernacle as consecrated Hosts [Eucharist] only when the lamp is lit.

Appendix B – A Vision of Hell

Today, I was led by an Angel to the chasms of hell. It is a place of great torture; how awesomely large and extensive it is! The kinds of tortures I saw: the first torture that constitutes hell is the loss of God; the second is perpetual remorse of conscience; the third is that one's condition will never change; the fourth is the fire that will penetrate the soul without destroying it – a terrible suffering, since it is purely spiritual fire, lit by God's anger; the fifth torture is continual darkness and a terrible suffocating smell, and despite the darkness, the devils and the souls of the damned see each other and all the evil, both of others and their own; the sixth torture is the constant company of Satan; the seventh torture is horrible despair, hatred of God, vile words, curses and blasphemies. These are the tortures suffered by all the damned together, but that is not the end of the sufferings. There are special tortures destined for particular souls. These are the torments of the senses. Each soul undergoes terrible and indescribable sufferings, related to the manner in which it has sinned. There are caverns and pits of torture where one form of agony differs from another. I would have died at the very sight of these tortures if the omnipotence of God had not supported me. Let the sinner know that he will be tortured throughout all eternity, in those senses which he made use of to sin. I am writing this at the command of God, so that no soul may find an excuse by saying there is no hell, or that nobody has ever been there, and so no one can say what it is like.

I, Sister Faustina, by the order of God, have visited the abysses of hell so that I might tell souls about it and testify to its existence. I cannot speak about it now; but I have received a command from God to leave it in writing. The devils were full of hatred for me, but they had to obey me at the command of God. What I have written is but a pale shadow of the things I saw. But I noticed one thing: that most of the souls there are those who disbelieved that there is a hell. When I came to, I could hardly recover from the fright. How terribly souls suffer there! Consequently, I pray even more fervently for the conversion of sinners. I incessantly plead God's mercy upon them. O my Jesus, I would rather be in agony until the end of the world, amidst the greatest sufferings, than offend You by the least sin.

[The above is taken from Diary, 741 from Notebook II of "Diary of Saint Faustina Kowalska: Divine Mercy in My Soul", pp. 296-297, © 1987, Marian Press, Stockbridge, MA, ISBN 978-0-944203-04-0].

Appendix C – Once saved, always saved? Let's ask Jesus

Question #3: How do I get to Heaven?, discussed the need for a life-long pursuit of Faith: a life of striving to know, love, and serve God. To know God by having a personal relationship with Jesus Christ (through **pray**er and Biblical **read**ings); to love God by **obey**ing His commandments (the 10 Commandments, plus the 5 Precepts of the Catholic Church – that which includes meeting Jesus in the Eucharist and Reconciliation); and to serve God by loving your neighbor through good works called **charity**.

Pray–**R**ead–**O**bey–**C**harity: The life-long process – PROC – for getting to Heaven.

What did Jesus say about being saved?

"Whoever believes and is baptized will be saved ..." – Jesus [Mk. 16:16]

Point 1➜ Mark 16:16 does *not* contain the phrase "is saved", which implies a *discrete* moment in time, like "once saved, always saved". Jesus said "will be saved", because He requires of us a *continuous* pursuit of well-formed Faith, just like St. Paul said in Philippians 2:12: "...*work out* your salvation with fear and trembling". (Italics added) The Old Testament phrase "with fear and trembling" means "with awe and seriousness in the service of God".

Point 2➜ "Believes" is a pregnant word; it means "trust in God and His truths" and "obey His commandments". While "trust in God and His truths" is discrete belief, the phrase "obey His commandments", said by Jesus in Matthew 19:17: "...if you wish to enter into life, keep the commandments", is a continuous process because the word "keep" means "to continue in an action".

The phrase, "is baptized" means "born of water and the Spirit", said Jesus in Jn. 3:5: "Amen, amen, I say to you, no one can enter the kingdom of God without being born of water and Spirit". The "born of water" phrase is the discrete process of being baptized in water, whereas "[baptized in] the Spirit" is a continuous process of living out your life imitating Christ. This includes being God's witness (e.g., doing the Works of Mercy) and evangelizing others (Jesus' Great Commission for us: "Go, therefore, and make disciples of all nations, baptizing them in the name of the Father, and of the Son, and of the Holy Spirit, teaching them to observe all that I have commanded you. And behold, I am with you always, until the end of the age." (Matt. 28:19-20)). Being God's witness and evangelizing others imply actions of love toward our neighbor. The latter aligns with Jesus' new commandment: "I give you a new commandment, that you love one another. Just as I have loved you, you also should love one another." [John 13:34]. Three (paraphrased) Biblical references especially remind us that Jesus' new commandment must be put into action in our lives:

Matthew 25:31-46 ➜ Jesus' *Judgment of the Nations*
Revelation 3:16 ➜   *...if you are lukewarm, I [Jesus] will spit you out of my mouth.*
James 2:26 ➜   *...faith without works is dead.*

Conclusion: Did Jesus ever say "once saved, always saved"? You decide.

Acknowledgments

To Peter Riili – the most meticulous person that I have ever met, and the man who single-handedly caused me to write this book by introducing me to a brief-case of Lighthouse Catholic Media CDs: I appreciate your 100+ hours of book draft reviewing. I appreciate your editorial talents and the Catholic knowledge that you applied to this work. You also examined every word in the book. Proof? Finding and correcting my error on Mr. Flew's first name: 'Anthony' was corrected to 'Antony'. Now that's due diligence!

To Rebecca Norman, a Picatinny Arsenal, New Jersey (NJ), Christian colleague and Arsenal bandmember: you adeptly added details to the 10 Commandments list, removed content redundancy, and improved my grammar throughout. Thank you, and well done.

To Michael Maute, an 8-year U.S. marine, who ran into me at the water cooler [I barely survived] and willingly engaged in a discussion on God and the Bible: you are responsible for significantly improving my book Topic #1, *The Resurrection of Jesus Christ*, by forcing me to read another book on the life of Jesus in order to advance the evidence and case for Christ. I am indebted to you be-cause this topic is the most crucial one in the book. Thank you, Michael, and thank you for your long military service to our country. You're 'Semper Fidelis'!

To Walter Horzepa, a 16-year CCD teacher of Catholic doctrine: I am so grate-ful for your Catholic mind dumps spread across my whole book. Each page of doctrine that you offered up allowed me to pick the best ideas and sprinkle them into key book crevices. What an important reviewer you were. You filled in many verbal potholes. You definitely made the book truer to God's Word.

To Diane Francis, a 23-year Catholic CCD teacher and 16-year CCD Program Director at Sts. Peter and Paul Church, in Great Meadows, NJ: You read my manuscript and gave me encouragement and provided comments that allowed me to tone down some of the math details in the book. You therefore made the book more readable to the general public – crucial! See you in fall, 2021, when we begin the new Youth Ministry and continue teaching Confirmation classes.

To Mark Francis, my former co-coach in both boy's baseball and basketball, and a former assistant prosecutor in Warren County, NJ: you were responsible for pointing me to Lee Strobel's *The Case for Christ* book, one that improved my book Topic #1.

To Sister Theresa Marie Yeakel, who has given God more than 70 years of service: you improved key Catholic topics throughout the book. You shared your deep Catholic knowledge, apt analysis, and bold thoughts to propel this book to a much higher level. What a blessing to me having you on the editorial team. I hope that you, Sister Theresa, continue to have fine health and many more years of service to those in need. What a role model you are for us all.

To the following pixabay.com graphic artists and photographers, I thank you for your generosity in contributing images to this book: Clker-Free-Vector-Images, Suanpa, skeeze, tookapic, jesus12286, Alois Grundner, mohamed_hassan on Facebook, and PublicDomainPictures. And, for the use of one other image, I also thank: global justice by Vectors Point from the Noun Project.

To Rick Seiler, my book cover designer: this is the second project in which I enlisted your help. I am pleased with your graphic designs, and they have always been delivered in a pleasant and professional manner. Well done!

To Eileen Seiler, owner of frāze, LLC, a company that provides businesses and organizations with professional freelance writing, editing and proofreading services: you sprinkled pith, efficiency, and logic in key spots throughout my book. You delivered to me a much cleaner product, and I am very pleased. Thank you for preparing this book for nihil obstat and imprimatur consideration (obtained in June, 2020!) by the Catholic Church.

To Rev. John G. Hillier, Ph. D., who is Director of the Office of Pontifical Mission Societies, Director of the Office for Persons with Disabilities, Censor Librorum in the Diocese of Metuchen, a regular columnist to *The Catholic Spirit*, and author of the books, "Anecdotes & Scripture Notes for All Occasions" and "Breathing Life into the Church: Making Sense of Vatican II": thank you for reviewing my book in consideration for the Imprimatur and Nihil Obstat through the Diocese of Metuchen.

References

I chose not to include citations within this book. But you can find all 682 references and bibliographies (and the 72 Lighthouse Catholic Media® CDs that I listened to five-times-each, which blew out 3 car audio players) at website: **brianyoung.charity**

INDEX

About the Author

Brian Young has provided youth instruction for decades in areas of religion, music, math, chess, scouting, sports, and life skills. He currently is in his tenth year teaching Catholic Confirmation students and plans to start a youth ministry. His earlier interests included bicycling, hiking the Appalachian Trail, producing Gong Shows to benefit the homeless, tutoring math students to benefit food banks, and playing euphonium for the Salvation Army.

Young is a retired software programmer (his most proficient computer language: profanity – which triggered frequent trips to the confessional). He now plans to spend years engaging and encouraging world youth and the young at heart to live out their Catholic faith on the revealed 8 Streets to Christ. He and his wife, Anne, have one son and identical twin daughters.